FINDING A SCHOOL FOR YOUR CHILD IN
SAN FRANCISCO & MARIN

Printed in the United States

Cover and text design created
and produced on computer by
Dare Porter / Real Time Design,
Oakland, CA

Library of Congress Cataloging-in-Publication Data
Finding a school for your child in San Francisco & Marin / David Denman . . .
[et al.].
p. cm.
ISBN 0-87701-738-7
1. Private schools—California—San Francisco—Directories.
2. Private schools—California—Marin County—Directories.
3. Public schools—California—San Francisco—Directories.
4. Public schools—California—Marin County—Directories.
I. Denman, David.
L903.C25S264 1990
371'.01'02579461—dc20   90-33953
                                                CIP

10 9 8 7 6 5 4 3 2 1

Chronicle Books
275 Fifth Street
San Francisco, California 94103

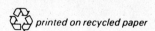 printed on recycled paper

FINDING A SCHOOL
FOR YOUR CHILD IN
SAN FRANCISCO & MARIN

•••••••••••••••••••••••••••••••••

David Denman

Vera Obermeyer

Virginia Reiss

Suzanne Warren

Chronicle Books • San Francisco

We acknowledge
with appreciation:
Svein Arber, publisher
of the previous edition of
Finding a School for
Your Child in San
Francisco and Marin;
our editor Bill LeBlond
of Chronicle Books,
for his encouragement
and trust; Cheryl Tsang,
who made the maps
of the private schools
of San Francisco;
our families and friends
for their support,
patience, and under-
standing while
this project was
underway.

Contents

The authors acknowledge,
with appreciation and
respect, the dedication of
the teachers in San Francisco
and Marin who devote such
energy, expertise, and love
to the education of all
our children.

Introduction

■■■■■■■■■■■■■■■■■■■■■■■■■■■■■■■

IN SEARCH OF THE RIGHT SCHOOL
1990 Revision

Since the publication of **Finding A School for Your Child in San Francisco and Marin** in 1984, many changes have occurred in Bay Area school systems. A few schools have closed their doors; several have new principals or directors or locations; and, inevitably, tuition fees have increased.

A notable change is the "open enrollment" policy of the San Francisco Unified School District. This program enables students to attend any public school in the City for which they are qualified, if there is space available. Thus, the public school choices in San Francisco are more numerous and the public school section of this new edition is considerably more extensive. Finding the "right" school for your daughter or son is now even more challenging – as you have even more options. (The growth of this new edition has necessitated the addition of two authors: Virginia Reiss and David Denman, two experienced educational consultants.)

As a way of beginning your search for the right school, ask yourself what kind of environment, as well as what kind of education, you want for your son or daughter. This is an important preliminary question – which suggests others. Does the "head of school" exhibit the qualities you want for your child? Does the school have a strict, hierarchical structure, with a principal who is autocratic? Or is the school more loosely structured with a principal who lets the rules and life of the school evolve with the needs of the teachers and students? Does the structure of the school lie somewhere in between these extremes? Do the school's values reflect your own? Do the adults at the school seem to be the kind of mentors and role models you want for your child?

In one way or another, are parents expected to become actively involved? Do *you* want to play an active part in the life of the school? Or would you prefer to be less involved in your child's schooling? Will you need before and after school care of your child in order to accommodate your schedule? These are preliminary questions which you need to ask yourself as you embark on selecting the right school for your child. They are as important, if not more so, than more objective questions. Other preliminary questions include: public or private school? nonsectarian or parochial? single sex or coed school? general education or special education?

How do you find out about prospective schools for your child? Obviously, we think this book will be helpful in a very basic way. The "Cross Index of Schools and Services" will be helpful in identifying specific aspects of a school, or in identifying schools which meet particular criteria. In addition, a map has been included to help you locate each school. Of course, you will also obtain information from other sources: recommendations from friends and acquaintances; talks with students who have attended these schools; descriptive brochures (which are obtainable by calling each school); and, finally, school visitations.

The first step in your search should be a visit to your child's assigned public school. Our guess is that you will find a dedicated principal and caring teachers. Get to know the principal. Request to sit in on two or three different classes and spend as much time as you can learning about the school. You will come away with some important observations, impressions, and conclusions by which to measure other schools you decide to consider. Then ask yourself how far from home you are willing to send your child; how much the family can afford to pay for tuition and, if needed, for supplemental day care. Then visit other schools that especially interest you, fully prepared with specific questions, such as the following:

1) What is the educational philosophy of the school? Ask to have the goals and curriculum described.

2) What is the discipline policy? Are uniforms required? If not, is there a dress code?

3) In the case of an elementary school, are there openings after the first year of that particular school? Is it possible, for example, to enter a child in third grade, or are chances slim after kindergarten?

4) What is the current enrollment? The anticipated future enrollment?

5) What is the training and experience of the teachers?

6) What is the teacher–student ratio? What is the staff turnover each year?

7) Are there provisions for tutoring or for other special needs? Is counseling

available?

8) How individualized is the program?

9) What is the school calendar? Are there special holidays and vacations?

10) What are the school hours? Is extended day care available? At what cost?

11) What arrangements are available for paying tuition?

12) Is financial aid available? Are these awards based upon need and/or merit? Are loans as well as grants available?

13) How does the school report on the child's progress? Are there report cards, conferences, or both?

14) What is the policy regarding parent visits to the classroom during the school year?

15) Does the school have a list of schools/colleges recent graduates have gone on to?

16) What is the policy on homework?

17) Does the school have a special emphasis or unique orientation? Examples would include programs such as drama, music, bilingual education, fine arts, backpacking, or any special features that the school considers integral to its curriculum.

18) What extra-curricular activities are available?

19) Does the school schedule field trips? Examples?

20) Is there food service?

21) What level of parent involvement is expected?

22) Is transportation provided? If not, are carpools available?

Observe the physical plant, playground, lunchroom, auditorium, and gymnasium. Make sure to see the library and the computer facilities. Visit appropriate classrooms with your child. (You should be aware that the teachers you observe may not have your child in class next year; the overall "feel" of the school is as important as the approach of a particular teacher.) Pay close attention to the interaction of teachers and students. Are the students stimulated and involved? Also, try to get a feeling for the attitudes of the students toward each other. Would your child be comfortable in this atmosphere?

When you leave the school, ask yourself whether or not it is still on your list. If it is, resist the temptation to say, "This is it." You won't really know what you think or how you feel about one school until you've had a chance to compare and contrast it with others.

You may be feeling overwhelmed at this point. Choosing a school for your child can be an exciting learning experience for you and your family. However, as you begin zeroing in on the "right" school, you will gain the satisfaction of knowing you are making a carefuly planned, informed decision.

And if all else fails, don't despair. The authors are available as consultants.

Timeline

Begin your search for a school in the Fall, a year before your child is to start in a new school. In San Francisco, call or visit the San Francisco Unified School District Student Assignment Office, 170 Fell Street, Room 10A, San Francisco, CA 94102, telephone: (415) 241-6085. Students are assigned according to the home address of the parent or legal guardian, approved Optional Enrollment Requests (OERs), or special program placements (for children with special education needs). Pre-registration begins around November 1 each year. If you want your child to attend a school other than one assigned on the basis of home address, an Optional Enrollment Request form must be submitted between early November and early January. The OER must be submitted in person to the first choice school or the Student Assignment Office. Approval of OERs is based on space availability, racial, and ethnic guidelines. Only parents and children moving into San Francisco after the January due date may submit late OERs.

For San Francisco private schools, applications generally close January 10 - 20; parent notification is around March 10 - 15. Some schools have openings and accept eligible students any time of the year.

For many private schools in Marin, the application deadline is March 1. However, parents should begin their application process in the Fall to avoid missing individual school deadlines. Many schools accept students who meet their admission requirements on a space-available basis throughout the year.

CROSS INDEX
OF PRIVATE SCHOOLS AND SERVICES

■■■■■■■■■■■■■■■■■■■■■■■■■■■■■■

While each private school has its own unique "personality," the search for one that will fit most closely the needs of a particular individual begins with a sorting process. The following section is designed to make that sorting process easier.

All independent schools listed in this book are presented here on the left in alphabetical order, regardless of geographic location. At the right is the number of the page where one can find a fuller description of each school. Other important information follows. At a glance the reader will find such pertinent facts as the size of the school, the ages and grades served, whether or not summer or special education services are available, its religious affiliation—if it has one—and whether it accepts boys only, girls only, or is coeducational.

Though this menu is not the full "meal," the authors hope that those schools that contain specific features important for a particular child will be more easily targeted.

CROSS INDEX OF PRIVATE SCHOOLS AND SERVICES

Adda Clevenger Junior Preparatory and Theater School for Children

Allaire School

Archbishop Riordan High School

Big City Montessori School

Binet-Montessori School

Brandeis-Hillel Day School (Marin)

Brandeis-Hillel Day School (S.F.)

Branson School

Bridgemont High School

Burt Center

Cascade Canyon School

Cathedral School for Boys

Challenge to Learning

Child Center

Children's Circle Center

Children's Day School

Children's School of San Francisco

Christian Life School

Page	County	Grades Served (or Ages)	Size of Student Body	Coed	Girls Only	Boys Only	Special Education Services Offered	Summer Programs Offered	Religious Affiliation (other than Catholic)	Roman Catholic	Montessori	Day Care Offered
41	S.F.	K-8	504	•				•				
119	M.	1-8	12	•			All	•				
42	S.F.	9-12	650		•					•		
43	S.F.	PreK-K	75	•				•			•	•
43	S.F.	PreK-3	120	•				•			•	•
120	M.	K-6	105	•					•			•
44	S.F.	1-8	272	•					•			
121	M.	9-12	320	•				•				
45	S.F.	6-12	80	•					•			
46	S.F.	Ages 3-10	24	•			All	•				•
122	M.	K-8	20	•				•				
47	S.F.	K-8	200		•			•	•			•
48	S.F.	Ages 11-21	36	•			All	•				
123	M.	Ages 6-18	18	•			All	•				
124	M.	PreK-3	80	•				•				
49	S.F.	Ages 2-6	140	•				•				•
50	S.F.	K-6	24	•				•			•	
125	M.	PreK-9	320	•					•			•

CROSS INDEX OF PRIVATE SCHOOLS AND SERVICES

Convent of the Sacred Heart Elementary School

Convent of the Sacred Heart High School

Cornerstone Academy

Discovery Center School

Drew College Preparatory School

Ecole Notre Dame des Victoires

Edgewood Children's Center

Edgewood Day Treatment Program

Erikson School

Fellowship Academy

French American International School

Hamlin School

Hebrew Academy of San Francisco

Hergl School

Hillwood Academic Day School

Holy Name of Jesus School

Immaculate Conception Academy

International Christian School

	Page	County	Grades Served (or Ages)	Size of Student Body	Coed	Girls Only	Boys Only	Special Education Services Offered	Summer Programs Offered	Religious Affiliation (other than Catholic)	Roman Catholic	Montessori	Day Care Offered
	51	S.F.	PreK -6	370		•			•		•		•
	51	S.F.	9-12	200		•					•		
	52	S.F.	Ages 3-12	300	•				•	•			•
	53	S.F.	K-8	350	•				•				•
	54	S.F.	9-12	100	•				•				
	55	S.F.	K-8	312	•				•		•		•
	56	S.F.	Ages 6-12	36	•			All	•				•
	57	S.F.	Ages 3-11	30	•			All	•				•
	58	S.F.	Ages 8-11	22	•			All	•				
	59	S.F.	K-8	185	•					•			•
	60	S.F.	PreK -12	450	•								•
	61	S.F.	K-6	335		•							•
	62	S.F.	PreK -12	190	•								•
	62	S.F.	Ages 4-21	10	•			All	•				•
	64	S.F.	K-8	125	•				•				•
	65	S.F.	K-8	514	•				•			•	•
	66	S.F.	9-12	300		•					•		
	66	S.F.	PreK -7	325	•				•	•			•

CROSS INDEX OF PRIVATE SCHOOLS AND SERVICES

Jamestown Learning Center

Kaleidoscope School

Katherine Delmar Burke School

Katherine Michiels School

Kittredge School

Lakeside Presbyterian Center for Children

La Mel School

Laurel School

Leebil School

Lick-Wilmerding High School

Live Oak School

Lycee Francais French School

Lycee Francais International

Maria Montessori School of the Golden Gate

Marin Academy

Marin Catholic High School

Marin Country Day School

Marin Horizon School

	Page	County	Grades Served (or Ages)	Size of Student Body	Coed	Girls Only	Boys Only	Special Education Services Offered	Summer Programs Offered	Religious Affiliation (other than Catholic)	Roman Catholic	Montessori	Day Care Offered
	67	S.F.	Ages 12-21	24	•			All	•				•
	126	M.	PreK -1	36	•								
	68	S.F.	K-8	360		•			•				•
	69	S.F.	PreK -2	80	•				•				•
	70	S.F.	1-8	103	•				•				•
	71	S.F.	Ages 2-6	140	•			Some	•				•
	72	S.F.	Ages 4-21	75	•			All	•				
	73	S.F.	PreK -9	100	•				•				•
	127	M.	9-12	15	•			All	•				
	74	S.F.	9-12	330	•				•				
	75	S.F.	K-6	105	•				•				•
	76	S.F.	PreK -12	275	•				•				•
	127	M.	PreK -12	350	•								•
	77	S.F.	Ages 1.5-12	60	•			Some	•			•	•
	128	M.	9-12	285	•				•				
	129	M.	9-12	180	•						•		
	130	M.	K-8	475	•				•				
	131	M.	PreK -8	180	•				•			•	•

CROSS INDEX OF PRIVATE SCHOOLS AND SERVICES

Marin Primary School

Marin School for Learning

Marin Waldorf School

Mercy High School

Montessori House of Children

Morrisania West, Inc. (S.F. Postal Street Academy)

Mother Goose School

Mount Tamalpais School

New Learning School

North Bay Marin School

Oakes Children's Center

One Fifty Parker Street School

Open Book School

Open Door Christian School

Pacific Primary School

Phoenix Academy

Presentation High School

Presidio Hill School

Page	County	Grades Served (or Ages)	Size of Student Body	Coed	Girls Only	Boys Only	Special Education Services Offered	Summer Programs Offered	Religious Affiliation (other than Catholic)	Roman Catholic	Montessori	Day Care Offered
132	M.	PreK-5	200	•			Some	•				•
133	M.	PreK-12	12	•			All					•
134	M.	K-8	165	•								
78	S.F.	9-12	600		•			•		•		
78	S.F.	Ages 2-8	100	•				•			•	•
79	S.F.	9-12	44	•				•				
80	S.F.	Ages 2-7	110	•				•				•
135	M.	K-8	240	•								•
81	S.F.	6-12	90	•				•				
136	M.	6-12	90	•				•				
82	S.F.	Ages 4-13	20	•			All	•				
83	S.F.	Ages 2-6	60					•				•
83	S.F.	Ages 8-13	18	•			All	•				
137	M.	PreK-6	148	•					•			•
84	S.F.	Ages 2-6	81	•				•				•
85	S.F.	PreK-12	50	•				•				•
86	S.F.	9-12	305		•					•		
87	S.F.	K-8	90	•								•

CROSS INDEX OF PRIVATE SCHOOLS AND SERVICES

Real School

Rivendell School

Sacred Heart Cathedral Preparatory

Sacred Heart Grammar School

St. Anselm's School

St. Anthony's School

St. Dominic School

St. Emydius School

St. Gabriel Parish School

St. Hilary School

St. Ignatius College Preparatory School

St. John's Elementary School

St. John Ursuline High School

St. Joseph School

St. Mark's School

St. Monica School

St. Paul's High School

St. Paulus Lutheran School

	Page	County	Grades Served (or Ages)	Size of Student Body	Coed	Girls Only	Boys Only	Special Education Services Offered	Summer Programs Offered	Religious Affiliation (other than Catholic)	Roman Catholic	Montessori	Day Care Offered
	138	M.	K-8	28	•				•				•
	88	S.F.	K-6	60	•				•				•
	88	S.F.	9-12	950	•						•		
	89	S.F.	K-8	200	•						•		•
	139	M.	K-8	150	•						•		•
	90	S.F.	K-8	300	•						•		•
	91	S.F.	K-6	195	•						•		
	91	S.F.	K-8	220	•						•		
	92	S.F.	K-8	435	•			Some			•		•
	140	M.	K-8	243	•				•		•		
	93	S.F.	9-12	1240	•				•		•		
	94	S.F.	K-8	270	•				•		•		•
	95	S.F.	9-12	166		•					•		
	95	S.F.	K-8	287	•						•		•
	140	M.	K-8	315	•				•		•		•
	96	S.F.	K-8	336	•				•		•		•
	97	S.F.	9-12	180		•					•		
	98	S.F.	PreK -8	171	•				•	•			•

CROSS INDEX OF PRIVATE SCHOOLS AND SERVICES

St. Raphael's School

St. Rita's School

St. Thomas the Apostle School

San Domenico Early Education School

San Domenico Lower School

San Domenico High School

San Francisco Chinese Parents' Committee School

San Francisco Day School

San Francisco Hearing and Speech Center

San Francisco Junior Academy

San Francisco School

San Francisco University High School

San Francisco Waldorf School

Sandpaths Academy

Sky's the Limit

Sparrow Creek Montessori School

Star of the Sea School

Sterne School

	Page	County	Grades Served (or Ages)	Size of Student Body	Coed	Girls Only	Boys Only	Special Education Services Offered	Summer Programs Offered	Religious Affiliation (other than Catholic)	Roman Catholic	Montessori	Day Care Offered
	141	M.	K-8	250	•				•		•		•
	142	M.	K-8	210	•						•		•
	99	S.F.	K-8	255	•						•		•
	143	M.	PreK -K	70	•						•		•
	144	M.	1-8	177	•						•		•
	146	M.	9-12	150		•					•		
	100	S.F.	PreK -6	200	•				•				
	101	S.F.	K-8	369	•				•				•
	102	S.F.	Ages 3-10	14	•			All					
	103	S.F.	K-10	116	•					•			
	104	S.F.	PreK -8	207	•				•			•	•
	105	S.F.	9-12	385	•				•				
	105	S.F.	K-8	186	•				•				•
	106	S.F.	Ages 3-21	26	•			All	•				
	147	M.	Ages 6-14	20	•			All	•				
	148	M.	PreK -K	22	•							•	
	107	S.F.	K-8	300	•							•	•
	108	S.F.	6-12	60	•			All	•				

CROSS INDEX OF PRIVATE SCHOOLS AND SERVICES

Stuart Hall for Boys

Sunny Hills

Synergy School

Tam Creek School

Timothy Murphy School

Town School

Urban School of San Francisco

West Portal Lutheran School

Wildshaw International School

Zion Lutheran School

Page	County	Grades Served (or Ages)	Size of Student Body	Coed	Girls Only	Boys Only	Special Education Services Offered	Summer Programs Offered	Religious Affiliation (other than Catholic)	Roman Catholic	Montessori	Day Care Offered
109	S.F.	PreK-8	290			•		•		•		•
148	M.	Ages 13-18	40	•			All					
110	S.F.	K-6	80	•				•				•
149	M.	PreK-5	50	•				•				•
151	M.	Ages 7-14	51			•	All	•				
111	S.F.	K-8	396			•		•				•
112	S.F.	9-12	175	•								
113	S.F.	K-8	560	•				•	•			•
114	S.F.	6-12	75	•				•				
114	S.F.	K-8	210	•					•			•

Kindergarten Readiness

A child's readiness for kindergarten is difficult to determine, and many parents can spend sleepless nights worrying about a child's early school years. With the advent of the "pushed down" curriculum (moving first grade curriculum to kindergarten), parents and teachers are beginning to see increased signs of stress and failure among primary grade students. As educators, we have seen an increase in the number of children falling behind their classmates academically, emotionally, or socially. These children often develop low self-esteem from the constant negative comparison to their more "successful" kindergarten peers.

Many parents have responded by waiting an extra year before enrolling their children in kindergarten and by relying on one of the variety of tests designed to determine kindergarten "readiness." Many schools have responded by slowing or reversing the trend for teaching more academic subjects, by establishing developmental kindergartens or two-year kindergartens, or by using older age requirements. In any event, an increasing number of parents and teachers appear to be signaling that a heavy academic curriculum is probably not appropriate for many of our four to five-year-old students. This view is solidly supported by recent research studies.

How can a parent decide if a child is ready to enter kindergarten? One of the guidelines is age. Individual children vary markedly in their rate of development, and many children change dramatically between the ages of four and five. Parents should consider specifically their child's language development, attention span, and motor development. "Immaturity" in these areas could be an early sign of potential learning problems, and perhaps kindergarten might aid in earlier identification and correction of such problems.

Consideration should also be given to the type of kindergarten. Is it highly academic, developmental, somewhere in the middle, or individualized? Is the classroom equipped to handle individual differences, and is the program flexible enough to meet a variety of needs?

Results of screening tests are valuable only when considered in the overall picture. **The results of one individual test given on one particular day** should not be used as the sole basis of decision. Finally, and most important, the observations of the preschool teachers, professionals, and parents are often the best indication of a child's readiness for a particular kindergarten.

Progress in kindergarten should be monitored frequently. Unhappiness or stress may be a clear indication that the school is inappropriate. Not all children respond well to all programs. In any case, the focus of any kindergarten program should be the development of a child's natural curiosity and love of learning.

Types of Schools

The following is a brief description of the types or categories of schools included in **Finding a School for Your Child in San Francisco and Marin**. Refer to the Appendix for the comprehensive listing of individual schools in each category.

MONTESSORI EDUCATION

Montessori schools follow the teaching principles of Maria Montessori, an Italian physician and educator who developed the educational system that bears her name. Montessori's teaching techniques depended on the use of manipulative devices that were designed to develop sensorimotor abilities. One important element of Montessori learning theory is that children go through certain periods of sensitivity in which they are particularly receptive to learning specific skills. To varying degrees, Montessori schools provide instruction consistent with Maria Montessori's philosophy.

ROMAN CATHOLIC EDUCATION

The Office of Catholic Schools of the Archdiocese of San Francisco provides educational services to all Catholic schools in San Francisco, Marin and San Mateo Counties. Parish schools are under the direction of the local pastor and principal; private Catholic schools are under the direction of the specific religious community that staffs them. The office of the Archdiocese of San Francisco, Office of Education, is at 443 Church Street, San Francisco, CA 94114, (415) 565-3660. The Superintendent of Catholic Schools is Sister Glenn Anne McPhee. She states that "the primary purpose of the Catholic schools is to provide a value-centered Christian education in the Catholic tradition. All Catholic schools are subject to the Statutes of the Archdiocese but have latitude in developing curriculum and standards."

Most Catholic schools are from kindergarten through grade eight and provide extended day care. Several have pre-kindergarten programs, a few begin in Grade One, and one school terminates at sixth grade. There are ten Roman Catholic secondary schools (grades 9 - 12) in San Francisco and two Roman Catholic secondary schools in Marin County supervised by the Archdiocese of San Francisco.

HOMESCHOOLING

For a variety of reasons, some parents in the Bay Area are currently teaching their children at home. Some parents believe that their children are not ready for the academic structures found in many schools. Some children may suffer from stress and burn out in the early grades. With homeschooling, the child may proceed at a comfortable rate and avoid the pressure to fit into a class of thirty peers.

Children are naturally curious, resourceful, and eager to learn. In the home environment, they can grow in a more relaxed setting, while receiving personalized attention that some parents believe is impossible to have in a classroom. Homeschooling is not limited to the home, for the children can be involved in music, dance, sports, drama, and after school activities. They often attend field trips with other homeschoolers.

Homeschooling involves a large commitment on the part of parents, but according to these parents, the rewards are great. Proponents believe that it is an opportunity to be fully involved in the education of their children.

Newsletters:
Growing Without Schooling, 2269 Massachusetts Ave., Cambridge, MA 02104. $20/6 issues.
Northern California Homeschool Association News, 3345 Santa Paula Dr., Concord, CA 94518. $15/6 issues (includes a list of Homeschooling contacts in Northern California).

Books to Read:
Teach Your Own by John Holt. Dell, 1982.
In Their Own Way by Thomas Armstrong. Tarcher, 1988.

SPECIAL EDUCATION

"Special" education is a term currently applied to those individualized services needed by some children in order to learn. Many children who require special education have a learning handicap, but special education also involves students with other types of disabilities such as hearing impairments, orthopedic handicaps, severe emotional disturbances, or visual handicaps.

The public schools must provide these services to all students regardless of the type and severity of their problems. Under Public Law 94-142, these services are to be provided at no cost to parents.

Some independent schools provide special education services as well. A wider spectrum of children may be able to receive these services privately since they do not always have to meet "eligibility standards" in order to demonstrate need. Because private schools deliver services according to their own philosophies, it is important to become familiar with the differences between schools before making a decision to enroll your child. Questions about the size and composition of the class and the diversity of the students served should be asked. It is important to know something of the training and experience of the staff, and how the graduates of these specialized programs fare when they move back into the "mainstream."

To learn of the services available in the Marin public schools, contact the Resource Specialist at the public school nearest your home.

In the San Francisco public schools, special education referral and information are available at the student's school of attendance. If your child is already identified as in need of special education, or you wish placement information, call the Special Education Department, (415) 241-6155. For the child with developmental disabilities or severe handicapping conditions not attending a S.F.U.S.D. program, parents should get in touch with S.F.U.S.D. Special Education Intake Unit, (415) 469-5703.

GIFTED PROGRAMS

GATE – Gifted and Talented Education – is the statewide public school program for gifted children that is offered both by the San Francisco Unified School District and through the Marin County Office of Education.

In the San Francisco public schools children are selected to participate in the program through an assessment process administered to all district second grade students or through an individual referral process for children above second grade. GATE programs begin in the third grade and continue through high school. In addition to a child's cognitive ability, creativity, leadership, and artistic aptitude are considered in program planning.

According to the S.F.U.S.D. brochure, "Elementary School Programs for GATE Students – 1988-9," "Students in all GATE classes are offered a broad range of activities which focus on higher order thinking skills, problem solving techniques, and creative inquiry and exploration through a variety of instructional strategies. Site plans and activities are based on student needs, the District curriculum and available resources."

For information about specific GATE programs in the San Francisco Unified School District, parents may contact the Gifted and Talented Education Program, 2550 25th Avenue, Room 12, San Francisco, CA 94116-2998; (415) 665-4939.

The Marin County contact person for the GATE program is John Rojas, Strawberry Point School, 117 East Strawberry, Mill Valley, CA 94941. For information call the Marin County Office of Education at (415) 499-5814. GATE classes in Marin County are offered from kindergarten through twelfth grade in most school districts. Individual districts have their own particular programs depending upon student and parental needs.

There are no private schools exclusively for gifted children in either San Francisco or Marin County. Selected private schools have accelerated curricula to meet the needs of gifted students.

Key to Abbreviations

CAIS	California Association of Independent Schools
CAPSES	California Association of Private Special Education Schools
CETA	California Employment Training Act
CHSPE	California High School Proficiency Examination
CTBS	Comprehensive Test of Basic Skills
ESL	English as a Second Language
GATE	Gifted and Talented Education
GED	General Educational Development Test and High School Equivalency
IEP	Individual Educational Plan
ISEE	Independent School Entrance Examination
LEAP	Learning Education and the Arts Program
LEP	Limited English Proficiency
NAES	National Association of Episcopal Schools
NAIS	National Association of Independent Schools
NCEA	National Catholic Educational Association
NIPSA	National Independent Private Schools Association
PL94-142	Education for all Handicapped Children Act of 1975
SAT	Scholastic Aptitude Test
SDC	Special Day Class
SFUSD	San Francisco Unified School District
SAT	Scholastic Aptitude Test
SSAT	Secondary School Admission Test
WAIS	Western Association of Independent Schools
WAPS	Western Association of Private Schools
WASC	Western Association of Schools and Colleges
WCEA	Western Catholic Educational Association

Section I
PRIVATE SCHOOLS

Listed Alphabetically

SAN FRANCISCO

MARIN COUNTY

Private Schools
SAN FRANCISCO

ADDA CLEVENGER JUNIOR PREPARATORY AND THEATER SCHOOL FOR CHILDREN

Mid-Sunset District, San Francisco, CA 94122

(415) 681-1140

•**Director:** Carol Harrison

Adda Clevenger Junior Preparatory and Theater School for Children, founded in 1980, is an academic, creative, and performing arts school. It has an enrollment of over 50 students in kindergarten through eighth grade. School hours are from 8:30 a.m. to 5:00 p.m. Extended care is available from 7:30 a.m. to 6:00 p.m. The school year is from September to mid-July, followed by an optional three-week summer day camp. Uniforms are required.

Registered with the California State Department of Education.

•**Philosophy/Goals/Curriculum:** The Adda Clevenger School was established to serve the needs of gifted and talented children. The philosophy of the school is best expressed by James J. Gallagher: "We can create giftedness through designing enriched environments and opportunities, or we can destroy it by failing to create those environments and opportunities. An environment has been designed to stimulate, challenge and inspire students, to open as many doors as possible and to provide opportunities to develop their talents to the fullest. By eighth grade, students should be well prepared to qualify for admission to honors classes in college preparatory high schools."

In addition to basic subjects, the curriculum includes Latin, history, classical and modern literature, geography, algebra, geometry, science, and moral philosophy. Students are placed in beginning, intermediate, or advanced classes, according to academic ability and motivation. All children participate in the creative and performing arts program which consists of creative writing, art, theater games, drama, chorus, ballet, and tap. The children also attend many live performances and do five or more shows of their own. The sports program includes soccer, track, swimming, and tennis.

•**Admission Requirements and Procedure:** Parents are invited to visit with the director. Following the visit, arrangements are made for the prospective student to attend classes for two full days. Testing may be required.

•**Most Recent Fee Schedule:** Tuition is $4,357 for a ten and one-half month school year, payable at $415 per month. Tuition policy allows a substantial family discount and some merit assistanceship for families with financial need.

ARCHBISHOP RIORDAN HIGH SCHOOL
175 Phelan Avenue, San Francisco, CA 94112
(415) 586-8200

•**Principal:** Father William A. O'Connell, S.M.

Riordan is a Catholic secondary school for young men, situated on an 11-acre site in the southwestern section of San Francisco. Under the tutelage of the Marianists, the school opened its doors in 1949. There is a dress code. Summer school is offered.

Accredited by WASC.

•**Philosophy/Goals/Curriculum:** "As a Catholic High School functioning in the 1980's, Riordan continues to engage its students in a process of education which promotes individual growth and emphasizes development in the spiritual, intellectual, social and physical aspects of life.

"Riordan strives to be a Christian community of faculty, students, parents, alumni and others who, by example, instruction and concern, mutually support and assist one another to develop the Christian values."

Course offerings include business education, creative arts, computer studies, English, foreign language, visual and performing arts, religious education, mathematics, science, physical education, and social studies. Programs are divided into three categories: honors, college preparatory, and general intensive instruction.

A wide range of extracurricular activities, clubs, and sports are available.

•**Admission Requirements and Procedure:** Applications are accepted beginning in October, following the annual Open House. Notification of freshmen acceptance begins in March.

•**Most Recent Fee Schedule:** Tuition: $3,450 per year, with a $250 registration/activity fee. There is a $40 application fee. Tuition can be paid over a ten-month period. Discount of $200 if paid in full before September 1. Financial assistance is available and can be applied for after acceptance and payment of Registration/Activity Fee.

BIG CITY MONTESSORI SCHOOL

240 Industrial Street (near Loomis), San Francisco, CA 94124

(415) 648-5777

•**Director:** Meighen Tideman

Big City Montessori School, formerly Westlake Montessori School, has been at its present site since February 1980. Big City serves children from preschool through kindergarten, ages two to six. Its enrollment is 75, with a teacher-student ratio of 1:12. All children attend 8:30 a.m. to 2:30 p.m., plus optional hours from 7:00 a.m. to 8:30 a.m. and from 2:30 p.m. to 6:00 p.m. Summer camp is conducted in August.

•**Philosophy/Goals/Curriculum:** "Big City Montessori School uses the Montessori curriculum and method, in which the teacher cultivates the child's natural powers. The environment is designed to attract and delight the child, as he handles the learning materials and meets the challenges they present. Through work the child finds and normalizes himself/herself."

•**Admission Requirements and Procedure:** Big City accepts children on a first come, first served basis. Most openings are available in June and September and should be applied for three to ten months ahead. The only children refused are those who suffer such severe physical or emotional handicaps that prevent their participation in the program.

•**Most Recent Fee Schedule:** Registration fee (nonrefundable): $65. Tuition, September through July school year: $3,985 per year. Extended care before and after school: $1.21 - $2.00 per hour, depending upon number of hours scheduled. Prepayment discounts are available.

BINET-MONTESSORI SCHOOL

1715 Octavia Street (at Pine), San Francisco, CA 94109

(415) 567-4000

•**Director:** Daniel J. Binet

Binet-Montessori School has been in existence since 1971. The school serves from preschool through third grade. Current enrollment is 120 students. Teacher-student ratio is 1:12. Teachers are Montessori trained. Handicapped children are accepted on an individual basis in consultation with appropriate professionals. School hours are from 9:00 a.m. to 3:00 p.m., with an extended day care program from 7:00 a.m. to 6:00 p.m. Binet-Montessori has a year-round program, with one-week vacations at the end of August and at Christmas.

Licensed by the State Department of Health.

• **Philosophy/Goals/Curriculum:** Binet-Montessori School adheres to the philosophy and curriculum of Maria Montessori.

• **Admission Requirements and Procedure:** Parents are invited to observe class in session during the week.

• **Most Recent Fee Schedule:** Tuition and Day Care: $430 per month.

BRANDEIS-HILLEL DAY SCHOOL

655 Brotherhood Way (between Lake Merced and 19th Avenue), San Francisco, CA 94115

(415) 334-9841

• **Director:** Fred S. Nathan
• **Principal:** Robert Foley

The Brandeis-Hillel Day School was founded in 1963. Its San Francisco branch conducts classes for kindergarten through eighth grade at the Frank and Jennie Gauss Campus at the above address. This facility includes – in addition to modern skylighted classrooms – a science laboratory, computer center, library, media center, gymnasium, and play areas. Enrollment is 272 students in grades one to eight. The teacher-student ratio is 1:14 for general classes and 1:10 for Hebrew. Teachers are credentialed. School hours are from 8:20 a.m. to 3:15 p.m. Extended day care is provided at the adjacent Brotherhood Way Jewish Community Center. Brandeis-Hillel maintains a second campus in Marin County (see page 120).

Accredited by CAIS and WASC. Affiliated with the Educational Records Bureau and the Bureau of Jewish Education, and a beneficiary of the Jewish Community Federation.

• **Philosophy/Goals/Curriculum:** "The philosophy of the school emerges from the Torah and Jewish tradition. The school creates a broad Jewish experience incorporating values and practices from varying traditions as they are relevant to contemporary life. The curriculum consists of general studies including language arts, reading, science, mathematics, social studies, computer science, physical education, dance, music and art; and Hebrew-Judaic studies, concentrating on the Hebrew language, the richness of Jewish history and literature, and the study of prayer, Torah and Talmud. Shabbat and the holidays are observed and celebrated, thus making living Judaism an integral part of the child's school experience. The focus is on meeting the individual needs of each child. Guiding each student to achieve his or her maximum potential and helping to achieve a positive self-image are the major objectives of the program."

•**Admission Requirements and Procedure:** Parents should call for an appointment. Admissions process includes filing an application and individual testing/ screening. Records of transfer students are reviewed by the Admissions Commitee.

•**Most Recent Fee Schedule:** Tuition: $2,750 per year plus a $150 supplementary fee, with a $250 reduction for siblings. Scholarships are available.

BRIDGEMONT HIGH SCHOOL

501 Cambridge (at Felton), San Francisco, CA 94134
(415) 333-7600

•**Academic Dean:** Jonathan L. Jones

Bridgemont High was founded in 1975. It has an enrollment of 80 students and serves students in grades six through twelve. The program is departmentalized with an average class size of ll.5 students. Teachers are credentialed or have advanced degrees. School hours are 8:15 a.m. to 2:45 p.m. There is a dress code.

Accredited by WASC.

•**Philosophy/Goals/Curriculum:** "Bridgemont High School is a coeducational, college-preparatory, non-denominational Christian school committed to academic excellence and to the development of sound character, grounded in a biblically-based value system. Professionally qualified faculty strive to provide personal attention to intellectual growth and academic success. Individual and group success through relationships, activities, and athletics is emphasized. Personal faith and development of God-given talents and abilities are nurtured through emphasis on personal involvement and commitment. The goal is a productive future built upon continued growth, and rich, supportive relationships."

•**Admission Requirements and Procedure:** There are two open houses for parents and students (Fall/Spring). Application forms, teacher recommendations, transcripts, and CTBS scores, along with character reference forms, are required as are a student interview and visit. Application deadline: January 19 for priority; on a rolling basis thereafter. Acceptance Notification Date: March 10 and thereafter.

•**Most Recent Fee Schedule:** Application Fee (all grades): $20. High school annual tuition: $2,450; High school fees (total): $510. Junior high annual tuition: $2,700; Junior high fees (total): $225. Sibling discounts are available. Financial aid is available based on need.

BURT CENTER

940 Grove Street (at Steiner Street), San Francisco, CA 94117
(415) 922-7700

•**Co-directors:** Mary C. Burt and Naomi Reichbach

Burt Center has been in existence since 1969 and at its present location since 1979. It is a day and residential treatment center serving emotionally disturbed children and young adults. The capacity of Burt Center is 24 children in both the 24-hour residential and day treatment programs. The age range is from three to ten at the children's campus. Primary professional staff consists of a clinical director, consulting child psychiatrist, pediatric medical director, consulting child psychologist, speech pathologist, social worker, education supervisor, residential supervisors, and teachers holding State Certification as specialists in education of severely educationally handicapped children. There is a residential staff-child ratio of 1:3, with classroom size varying from four to eight. The hours of the day program are from 9:00 a.m. to 3:00 p.m. Both the day and residential treatment programs operate on a year-round basis.

Licensed by the State Department of Health and accredited as a Psychiatric Treatment Center by the Joint Commission of Accreditation of Hospitals. Certified by the State Department of Education.

•**Philosophy/Goals/Curriculum:** "Burt Center utilizes a multi-disciplinary team to provide a psychodynamically-oriented treatment program. The objective is to assist the severely emotionally disturbed child to recover from catastrophic mental illness of childhood and to reach maximum potential for growth. Treatment procedures are individually planned for each child to bond to staff leading to eventual peer relationships. The treatment plan includes milieau therapy, therapeutic play sessions, psychotherapy, speech therapy, sensorimotor therapy, art, dance and music therapy as well as the day program."

•**Admission Requirements and Procedure:** The clinical team interviews the parents, reviews materials, and sees the child. The child should have had a "psychiatric, neurological or psychological evaluation with the diagnosis of childhood schizophrenia, psychosis, atypical behavior or severe behavioral disorder."

•**Most Recent Fee Schedule:** $2,300 per month for day program. $3,589 per month for residential treatment. Placements made through the Department of Social Services, Department of Mental Health, Regional Centers, and school districts.

CATHEDRAL SCHOOL FOR BOYS

1275 Sacramento Street (at Jones), San Francisco, CA 94108
(415) 771-6600

•**Headmaster:** Harry V. McKay, Jr.

Founded in 1957, Cathedral School for Boys is an Episcopal Day School for boys from kindergarten to eighth grade. Enrollment is 200, with 26 faculty members. No grade is larger than 24 students. School hours vary according to grade level. For boys in K - 4, an extended day program is available from 2:30 p.m. to 6 p.m. Uniforms are required.

Accredited by CAIS and member of NAIS, NAES.

•**Philosophy/Goals/Curriculum:** "The Cathedral School offers, within a Christian environment, a rich and challenging academic program for boys of various backgrounds from all over San Francisco. Boys are encouraged to put forth their best work in studies which combine intellectual challenge and creative expression. The single most important aspect of the school, however, is the unique emphasis that is placed on respect for each other. In the daily interaction of children and adults, the school strives to impart a sense of fairness, respect and tolerance. Teachers are selected for their academic strengths and interests, their experience in education, and their ability to inspire and encourage their students, as well as instruct them. The school believes that its student body must represent the diversity of the commumity it serves. One special element of the curriculum is the music studies program. Music theory and composition are taught as part of a musical education program. Additionally, boys in third grade may audition for membership in the Grace Cathedral Choir of Men and Boys."

•**Admission Requirements and Procedure:** An interview with the parents and tour of the school precedes an individual and group evaluation for kindergarten. Boys in grades one to eight are tested on the selected independent school testing day, and are expected to also make a classroom visit. Kindergarten applications are encouraged. The school is open to qualified boys of all religions.

•**Most Recent Fee Schedule:** Tuition ranges from $4,950 to $5,800, depending on grade level. Financial aid is available.

CHALLENGE TO LEARNING

924 Balboa Street (near 10th Avenue), San Francisco, CA 94118
(415) 221-9200

•**Director:** John S. Kainlauri
•**Assistant Director:** Kathi Rendon

Challenge to Learning School has been in existence since 1972. It has three programs: 1) The E.H. Program, serving the educationally handicapped, emotionally disturbed, and neurologially impaired from eleven to twenty-one years of age. (All teachers have special education credentials. An occupational therapist, speech pathologist and counselor/psychologist are on the staff.) 2) The tutorial program for junior and senior high school ages. 3) The computer education program for adults. E.H. Program hours are from 8:30 a.m. to 2:00 p.m. Tutorial sessions and computer classes are set up to meet students' schedules. CTL is open throughout the year.

Certified by the State Department of Education, CAPSES accredited, and licensed by the State Department of Social Services.

•**Philosophy/Goals/Curriculum:** "The E. H. Program is a highly structured, self-contained, and ungraded academic day program. The curriculum core is geared to meet the academic needs of each student. An individualized approach is used in teaching the basic skills. Emphasis is also placed on socialization experiences designed to develop appropriate social behavior." A wide variety of subjects is offered: social studies, science, life needs, enrichment, arts and crafts, typing, physical education, vocational and driver education.

The Tutorial Program serves the students attending public or private schools who are in need of specialized tutoring.

The Computer Program is geared to students who are seeking computer assisted instruction, training for GED and preparation for SAT and college admission tests. It also seves the needs of the re-entry adult to the work market in the full use of the computer.

• **Admission Requirements and Procedure:** Call or write the Director or Assistant Director. Submit psychiatric, psychological and educational evaluations, social, and medical history. Parent and student interview.

• **Most Recent Fee Schedule:** Students are funded in the E.H. Program through the school district. Scholarship assistance is available for private students.

CHILDREN'S DAY SCHOOL

333 Dolores Street (at 16th Street), San Francisco, CA 94110
(415) 861-5432

• **Director:** Jim Robinson

Children's Day School was founded in 1983 and has an enrollment of 140 children, two to six years of age. It has a toddler, preschool, and kindergarten/first grade program. School hours are 8:30 a.m. to 2:30 p.m., September through July, and extended care is offered from 7:30 a.m. to 8:30 a.m. and from 2:30 p.m. to 6:00 p.m. Summer care is provided during August. Limited parent participation is required.

Licensed by the State Department of Social Services and a member of the International Montessori Society.

• **Philosophy/Goals/Curriculum:** "Children's Day School is an eclectic blend designed to meet the needs of the Total Child. Children's physical, social, emotional and cognitive development is cared for on an equal basis. Children are not pushed and are encouraged to develop naturally at their own pace. Children's Day School has a progressive Montessori curriculum in addition to a major emphasis on all the arts, sciences and sensory-motor development. Classrooms are aesthetic, light and spacious, and the school is located on a one-acre oasis in the heart of San Francisco's sunbelt. There is a large vegetable garden, a farm with petting animals, lawn garden, climbing structures, a large sand playground, bicycles and safe, off street parking directly across from the historic Dolores Mission. Children are encouraged to play and learn in a peaceful atmosphere that will

nourish their self-esteem and build good, healthy foundations for their future."
•**Admissions Requirements and Procedure:** Admissions procedures consist of a
group orientation, a suggested classroom observation, filing of an application form,
followed by a personal interview. Children are not tested, but older preschoolers
and K - 1 children are asked to visit a classroom for the day to determine readiness
of the child for the school program. Classrooms are filled according to boy-girl
balance, age, and development.
•**Most Recent Fee Schedule:** Application fee: $35. Day school rates: $440
Toddler, $410 Preschool, and $415 Primary. Extended care: $125 per month. A
limited amount of scholarship aid is available.

THE CHILDREN'S SCHOOL OF SAN FRANCISCO

399 San Fernando Way (at Ocean Avenue), San Francisco, CA 94127
(415) 333-8683

•**Directors:** William Brunner and Katherine Carter
    "The Children's School of San Francisco has been incorporated as a non-profit
academic primary and elementary school since 1976. It features small classes with
individualized attention for each student. All teaching personnel have Bachelor's
degrees; most teachers have additional post-graduate education, such as Montessori training or Master's degrees in relevant fields. School hours are from 9:00 a.m.
to 3:30 p.m. Extended care is available from 7:45 a.m. before school, and until
6:00 p.m. after school. Summer school is offered with arts and crafts and other
day-camp activities, including trips to parks, beaches, museums and special
activities for children in the Bay Area."
    Licensed by the State Department of Health.
•**Philosophy/Goals/Curriculum:** "The school seeks to encourage children's
natural desire to learn about their world. The teaching fosters self-discipline and
cultivates curiosity in children by providing self-correction exercises and allowing
individual children in a single class to work at their own pace on subjects that
interest them at any given time. Gymnastics and swimming are included in a
complete physical education program. The school has a professional-quality
dramatic production theater. Children receive acting lessons and learn first-hand
about designing and sewing costumes, building scenery, and printing tickets and
playbills. Parents are invited to finished productions."

•**Admission Requirements and Procedure:** First come, first served.
•**Most Recent Fee Schedule:** $3,400 per academic year. Summer School
available weekly: $90.

CONVENT OF THE SACRED HEART ELEMENTARY SCHOOL
2222 Broadway (between Webster and Fillmore), San Francisco, CA 94115
(415) 563-2900

•**Co-heads:** Deborah Dumont and Agnes Rokitiansky
Founded in 1887, Convent of the Sacred Heart Elementary School is a school
for girls, with the exception of pre-kindergarten which is coed. It has a student
enrollment of 370, pre-kindergarten through eighth grades. Forty-six credentialed
teachers are on staff, with a teacher-student ratio of 1:14. School hours are 8:15
a.m. to 3:00 p.m.; extended day care is available until 6:00 p.m. A summer camp
program is provided. Uniforms are required.
Accredited by WASC and CAIS.
•**Philosophy/Goals/Curriculum:** A strong academic program is offered. The
curriculum includes reading, writing, spelling, grammar, mathematics, social
studies, science, foreign language, computer education, music, art, drama, physical
education, and outdoor education. Participation in the religious education
program is required. The services of a school counselor and an educational
therapist are available to the students.
•**Admission Requirements and Procedure:** Applications are accepted year-
round. Kindergarten screenings are in January and February. Applicants must
provide school records and recommendations. All applicants are interviewed.
•**Most Recent Fee Schedule:** Tuition is from $4,750 to $5,150 per year depending upon grade level. Additional fees are from $200 to $275 per year depending
upon grade level. Tuition loans and financial aid are available.

CONVENT OF THE SACRED HEART HIGH SCHOOL
2222 Broadway (between Webster and Fillmore), San Francisco, CA 94115
(415) 563-2900

•**Principal:** Leo J. Hogan
One of the three Schools of the Sacred Heart (see page 89), Convent of the

Sacred Heart High School was founded in 1887. A girls' school, it has 200 students in grades nine through twelve. There are 26 credentialed teachers, with average class size 15 students or less. School hours are from 8:30 a.m. to 3:10 p.m. A summer school program is provided.

Accredited by WASC and CAIS.

•**Philosophy/Goals/Curriculum:** The Schools of the Sacred Heart are bound with the other Sacred Heart schools across the country in their commitment to "Educating students to a faith which is relevant in a secularized world; developing a deep respect for intellectual values; instilling a social awareness which impels to action; building of community as a Christian value; fostering personal growth in an atmosphere of wise freedom."

The High School provides a vigorous college preparatory program, fulfilling University of California and private university requirements, as well as required theology/philosophy courses, while also offering challenging electives in fine and applied arts, social sciences, mathematics, English, science, and computer studies. Advanced Placement courses for college credit are offered in 14 subjects. The faculty, including lay and religious men and women, works to create a positive environment and a warm atmosphere within the school which encourages the development of leadership, self-confidence, and self-esteem in its young women.

•**Admission Requirements and Procedure:** Applications are accepted year-round. Applicants are tested in January; SSAT results are also accepted. Applicants must provide school records and recommendations, and they are interviewed.

•**Most Recent Fee Schedule:** Tuition for grades 9 through 11: $6,900; Tuition for grade 12: $7,000. Tuition loans and financial aid are available.

CORNERSTONE ACADEMY

1925 Lawton Street (at 25th Avenue), San Francisco, CA 94122
(415) 665-9747
801 Silver Avenue (at Cambridge St.), San Francisco, CA 94134

•**Principal:** Donald Langendorf
•**Executive Director:** Genevieve Lau

Cornerstone Academy, formerly Little Lights School, was founded in 1975 and is sponsored by the Cornerstone Evangelical Baptist Church. Three hundred children, ages three to twelve, are enrolled in preschool through eighth grade. The teacher-student ratio is 1:12. Teachers are credentialed. School hours are from 8:30 a.m. to 2:30 p.m. with extended care provided from 7:00 a.m. to 6:00 p.m. A summer school program is offered. Uniforms are required.

The preschool is licensed by the State Department of Social Services. The grade school is registered with the State Department of Education.

•**Philosophy/Goals/Curriculum:** The goal of the Cornerstone Academy program is to facilitate the children's mental, emotional, social, physical, and spiritual development. The preschool and kindergarten curriculum is bilingual (Cantonese Chinese and English); the grade-school curriculum has English as the medium of instruction and teaches Chinese as a second language. Character building, based on Christian principles, is an integral part of the school's program.

•**Admission Requirements and Procedure:** Admission is on a "first come, first served" basis in the preschool. Church members and siblings of enrolled children receive priority. After completion of an application form, parents attend an orientation meeting while grade school children are tested.

•**Most Recent Fee Schedule:** Preschool and kindergarten: $360 per month; Grades 1 to 8 (ten months): $200 per month; Extended care/Enrichment Program: $120 per month. Discount for siblings: $35 per month.

DISCOVERY CENTER SCHOOL

65 Ocean Avenue (at Alemany), San Francisco, CA 94112
(415) 333-6609

•**Director:** Kathleen Obar Cosgriff

Discovery Center School was founded in 1970. It has an enrollment of 350 students, kindergarten to eighth grade. Average class size is twenty, with twenty-five credentialed teachers on the staff. School hours are from 9:00 a.m. to 3:30 p.m., with extended day care available from 7:00 a.m. to 6:00 p.m. A summer program is provided from June through August.

Registered with the State Department of Education.

Accredited by NIPSA.

•**Philosophy/Goals/Curriculum:** "Discovery Center School is committed to the over-all development of the child. To this end, we provide strong instruction in the basic skills as well as a wide variety of cultural and aesthetic experiences within a success-oriented program. Because there are great differences among children of the same age, factors other than chronological age are considered in planning a program to meet the intellectual, social, emotional, and physical needs of the individual in the classroom. Computer-assisted instruction is integrated into the school program beginning in kindergarten, as well as a computer science program for grades five through eight. Foreign language instruction begins in third grade; art classes are provided weekly by an art specialist; there is a music program, a full-time physical education specialist instructor and an extra-curricular sports program at Middle School level. A librarian staffs a 6,000-volumn elementary school library."

• **Admission Requirements and Procedure:** An initial parent-child interview is followed by a review of the school records. A readiness test is required for entering kindergarten children. Prospective pupils are permitted to visit and participate in the classroom program. Acceptance is determined on the basis of class availability, personal interview, and prior school records.

• **Most Recent Fee Schedule:** Tuition: $2,950 per year (payable: $295 per month); Books and Materials Fee: $80 per year (payable: $40 per semester); Student Insurance: $8.50 per year; Computer Lab Fee (grades five through eight): $12.50 per month; Registration Fee (per child): $30; Music (optional): $16.50 per month (Registration Fee: $7.50). A 10 percent discount is provided for siblings.

DREW COLLEGE PREPARATORY SCHOOL

2901 California Street (at Broderick), San Francisco, CA 94115
2518 Jackson Street (at Steiner), San Francisco, CA 94115
(415) 346-4831

• **Principal:** James Henry

Drew is a college preparatory day school for grades nine through twelve. Drew was founded in 1908 and became particularly well known for preparing young men for the military academies. The academic program became completely college preparatory as well as coed in the 1960s. Total enrollment is 100 students; average class size is ten. A summer school program is provided. There is a special program of English for foreign students. Advanced Placement courses are available.

Accredited by WASC.

• **Philosophy/Goals/Curriculum:** "The philosophy of Drew is derived from its main function of preparing students for successful careers in college. While rules concerning attendance and assignments are strictly enforced and the tradition of scholarship is nurtured, at the same time within the school there is an easy give and take of ideas which is possible because of small classes and close rapport between student and teacher."

• **Admission Requirements and Procedure:** "Prior preparation and predictable ability to do the academic work required in college preparatory course. This includes English, mathematics, foreign languages, science and social science. Admission is based on previous grades, scores on standardized tests and recommendations from teachers and counselors. A two-hour test is required of all applicants unless a similar test has been taken within the last six months." An interview is arranged.

• **Most Recent Fee Schedule:** Tuition: $4,950 per year. A scholarship program is available for both entering and continuing students.

ECOLE NOTRE DAME DES VICTOIRES

659 Pine Street (between Grant and Stockton), San Francisco, CA 94108
(415) 421-0069

• **Principal:** Mrs. Mary Ghisolfo
Ecole Notre Dame Des Victoires was founded in 1924. It serves 312 students, kindergarten through eighth grade. Average class size is 35, with 12 credentialed teachers. School hours are from 8:35 a.m. to 3:15 p.m. Computer classes are offered during the summer. Uniforms are required.
Accredited by WASC.

• **Philosophy/Goals/Curriculum:** "N.D.V. provides a solid academic foundation in a Christian atmosphere. The highly trained and experienced staff responds to individual needs in a self-contained classroom setting. Formal religious instruction and a fundamental spirit of respect and service on the part of students, parents and teachers foster a shared community in which children learn and grow. As the School of the French National Church of San Francisco, N.D.V. provides daily French classes for all students. Programs and activities focusing on French culture are an integral part of the school curriculum."

• **Admission Requirements and Procedure:** Applications may be obtained from the school office. Interviews with the Principal commence in January for September admission. Both parents and children are expected to attend the interview, at which time a test is administered. Notification of status will be mailed by March 15. Families wishing to apply at other times of the year should call or write the school office for information.

•**Most Recent Fee Schedule:** Application Fee: $50; Archdiocesan Enrollment Fee: $125 per year; Textbook Rental Fee: $35; Mothers' Guild Dues: $35; Fathers' Guild Dues: $35; Tuition for one child: $1,850 per year; Tuition for two children: $3,400 per year; Tuition for three or more children: $4,350 per year. Kindergarten Fee: $350. Parish Pledge: $600. Scholarship program available.

EDGEWOOD CHILDREN'S CENTER

1801 Vicente Street (at 29th Avenue), San Francisco, CA 94116
(415) 681-3211

•**Executive Director:** Morris R. Kilgore
•**Director of Educational Services:** Paul E. Jobin

Edgewood was founded in 1851 as the San Francisco Orphan Asylum and has also been known as Edgewood Children's Home and the San Francisco Protestant Orphanage. It was renamed the Edgewood Children's Center in 1981. Edgewood Residential Treatment Program provides services to 36 boys and girls six through twelve years of age. Children are referred to the Center by the courts, social service agencies, hospitals, and schools because of severe behavioral, emotional, educational, or family problems. There are eight to nine students, a teacher, and an aide in each classroom. The four teachers are credentialed. There are also a limited number of day students. Art and shop programs are offered twice per week; a speech and language specialist and an occupational therapist are on staff. A complete summer school program is available.

Edgewood Children's Center is accredited by the Joint Commission for Accreditation of Hospitals, California Association of Services for Children.

•**Philosophy/Goals/Curriculum:** "The carefully structured residential program includes schooling, positive group living experiences and various modes of therapy for the child and other family members. The goal of this program is to return the child to a healthier home environment, or to a permanent substitute home after his or her stay at Edgewood. The mission of Edgewood is to take under its care

and charge children who may be homeless, friendless, needy, disturbed or handicapped, and to provide them with assistance which may include home, sustenance, education, care and treatment."
•**Admission Requirements and Procedure:** Referrals are usually made by schools, courts or social agencies.

EDGEWOOD DAY TREATMENT PROGRAM
(Formerly **Lucinda Weeks Center**)
2665 28th Avenue (at Vicente), San Francisco, CA 94116
(415) 664-7584

•**Director:** Barry Feinberg
    The Edgewood Day Treatment Program has been in existence since 1953 and associated with Edgewood Children's Center since 1979. It provides day treatment and comprehensive educational programming for 30 severely emotionally disturbed children from three and one-half to eleven years. The program is from 9:00 a.m. to 6:00 p.m., eleven months per year. Three meals a day and a snack are provided. The staff consists of three credentialed special education teachers, child care counselors, and specialists in art therapy, dance/movement/sensory/motor therapy, speech and occupational therapies. Clinical social work services are provided to children and families on a regular, on-going basis. Transportation is provided.
    Certified with the State Department of Education and licensed by the State Department of Social Services.
•**Philosophy/Goals/Curriculum:** "The full-day treatment program integrates special education, day care and clinical services to the child and his/her family. The operational orientation of the program is psychosocial/developmental. Goals are to establish a clear diagnostic picture of each child; to stabilize the child's behavior; to develop the child's learning capacities; to help the family function more effectively and adopt realistic expectations for their child; and to develop long term program plans for the family and child which will better enable the child to function successfully in a non-institutional environment."
•**Admission Requirements and Procedure:** Official referrals are initiated by the local school district.
•**Most Recent Fee Schedule:** No fees are assessed to families. The program is

funded by the local public school district, San Francisco Community Mental
Health Services, the Office of Child Development and private funding from
Edgewood Children's Center.

ERIKSON SCHOOL
333 Randolph Street (Arch Street), San Francisco, CA 94132
(415) 333-0440

• **Executive Director:** Shelly Lobell
• **Educational Director:** Greg Trevigne
   The Erikson School was founded in 1980. Twenty-two students, ages eight to
eleven, are enrolled, with a capacity of 28 students. Erikson School offers an
individualized instructional program for troubled and learning disabled adolescents, including group and individual instruction in the development of basic
skills and electives; structured activities; educational evaluation; vocational skills;
parent conferences and support groups. Teacher-student ratio in the basic
program is 1:4. School hours are 9:30 a.m. to 4:30 p.m. with specific hours
staggered according to individual needs. The school provides individual and group
therapy. Parents are required to attend monthly meetings. A July summer school
program is offered. Transportation is provided by the San Francisco Unified
School District.
   Registered with the State Department of Education.
• **Philosophy/Goals/Curriculum:** "The Erikson School is dedicated to developing
the educational and social skills of its students in a safe, warm, caring and highly
structured environment." Specific goals include providing a structured setting
where students are aware of expectations, responsibilities and rules; providing an
appropriate learning experience, and promoting academic and social progress. A
personalized program of instruction is planned with the goal of helping the student
attain appropriate levels of competence as well as to foster socio-emotional
development. The program focuses not only on the student's problem areas, but
also on areas of strength. Therefore, the program is viewed as being remedial,
therapeutic, developmental, and enrichment oriented."
• **Admission Requirements and Procedure:** Students must have a valid IEP
indicating eligibility for non-public school placement. Applicant and family must
partake in an initial interview and an intake process. Families may contact school

directly or be referred by schools, social services, or other community agencies.
•**Most Recent Fee Schedule:** Students are funded by school districts.

FELLOWSHIP ACADEMY

501 Cambridge Street (near Fenton), San Francisco, CA 94134
(415) 239-0511

•**Headmaster:** Reginald Nichols
Fellowship Academy, established in 1982, is a program of Fellowship Urban
Outreach. It serves kindergarten through eighth grade, with a student capacity of
185. Average class size is 18 - 20. Fourteen full-time and four part-time credentialed teachers are on staff. School hours are from 8:30 a.m. to 3:00 p.m., with
extended day care available from 7:00 a.m. until 6:00 p.m. Uniforms are mandatory. Parents are required to participate in ten hours of school projects and to join
the Parent Association.

Registered with the State Department of Education. Member of Association of
Christian Schools International.
•**Philosophy/Goals/Curriculum:** Fellowship Academy "has as its unique purpose
the blending of academic excellence with the molding of a desirable character,
and seeks to develop leadership skills. It aims to provide urban children with the
means to develop their potential to be all that they can be and to assist them in
the development of their leadership capabilities so that as adults they may provide
the guidance necessary to better the relational, intellectual and physical condition
of the urban community.

"Students will acquire new learning skills; develop self-esteem and moral
values; react positively to change; become aware of social responsibilities; appreciate their cultural heritage; understand that learning extends far beyond the borders
of the classroom; develop competence in basic skills; and be encouraged to fully
develop and exercise their leadership ability."

In addition to academics, the program includes computer instruction, foreign
language, and after school sports.
•**Admission Requirements and Procedure:** An application form is submitted
with a $20 nonrefundable fee; entrance tests are completed and supporting
documents received; an interview with parents and students conducted.
•**Most Recent Fee Schedule:** Kindergarten to fifth grade: $1,750 per year with a

$150 registration fee; Grades six to eight: $1,800 per year with a $200 registration fee. Tuition reduction for more than one child. Financial aid available.

FRENCH AMERICAN INTERNATIONAL SCHOOL

220 Buchanan Street (near Waller), San Francisco, CA 94102
(415) 626-8564

• **Head of School:** Alain Weber
• **Director of Admissions:** Edie L. Wexler

French American International School was founded in 1962. The school has 450 students from pre-kindergarten through twelfth grade. Average class size is 20. School hours are from 8:15 a.m. to 3:00 or 4:00 p.m. depending upon grade level. Extended day care is available until 6:00 p.m.

Accredited by WAIS and CAIS.

• **Philosophy/Goals/Curriculum:** The F.A.I.S. *Lower School's* (Pre-K to five) primary goal is "to create an effective learning center committed to understanding children's basic needs, a place where children may learn and grow in an atmosphere of affection, patience and positive expectations. The acquisition of the French language is achieved through an immersion program. By the end of grade five, students are functionally bilingual. . . . Specialty areas include music, art physical education and computer studies. Extra-curricular activities are available. The *Upper School* (six to twelve) provides an education directed toward a multinational equivalence, a universally accepted standard with access to major universities in the United States and other countries. Students obtain proficiency in language and mathematics. . . . Students become familiar with a subject in the field of human behavior and scientific inquiry, and acquire an appreciation of aesthetic and moral values. A third language is introduced in sixth grade. High School students participate in the International Baccalaureate or French Baccalaureate. Students may enter the high school in either the International Section or the French Section. No prior French experience is necessary to enter the International Section."

• **Admission Requirements and Procedure:** Primary and elementary level students are tested and a prior school recommendation is expected. Secondary students are admitted on the basis of academic records, SSAT or ISEE scores, recommendations or evaluations from two teachers, a student essay and a personal interview with the Director of Admissions. Besides academic potential, creativity and strong motivation are highly valued.

•**Most Recent Fee Schedule:** Tuition ranges from $5,200 to $6,200 per year depending upon grade level. The Application and Evaluation Fee is $50; and the Enrollment Fee is $250. Financial aid available based on need.

HAMLIN SCHOOL

2120 Broadway (between Webster and Buchanan), San Francisco, CA 94115
(415) 922-0300

•**Head:** Arlene Hogan

"As the first non-sectarian school for girls in California, Hamlin continues to provide a contemporary and academically challenging course of study for elementary school girls. Situated in Pacific Heights overlooking San Francisco Bay and the Marin Headlands, Hamlin reflects the diversity and traditions of San Francisco. There are currently 335 girls enrolled at the school which serves kindergarten through eighth grade. School hours are 8:20 a.m. to 1:30 p.m. for kindergarten students and 8:20 a.m. to 3:15 p.m. for older girls. There is an extended care program from 1:30 p.m. to 6:00 p.m. for children enrolled at the school, and an extensive after school activities program is also available. Uniforms are required."

Accredited by CAIS and NAIS.

•**Philosophy/Goals/Curriculum:** "The Hamlin School provides fine intellectual training to prepare its students for the challenges of secondary school and college. The program is designed to develop a strong foundation in basic skills, particularly in reading and mathematics. All students take art and music and daily physical education. There are competitive athletics for interested students in grades five through eight. French is offered in kindergarten through eighth grade and Latin in grades seven and eight. All school programs contribute to a balanced academic environment which allows each student to grow as an individual."

•**Admission Requirements and Procedure:** Kindergarten students visit the school and are evaluated for a developmentally appropriate placement. Older students are admitted by academic grades, placement tests, previous school records and a visit for the day.

•**Most Recent Fee Schedule:** Tuition ranges from $4,650 for kindergarten to

$6,150 for eighth grade. The fee for books, field trips and yearbooks is $275.

HEBREW ACADEMY OF SAN FRANCISCO

645 14th Avenue (Balboa), San Francisco, CA 94118

(415) 752-9583

•**Dean:** Rabbi Pinchas Lipner

The Hebrew Academy of San Francisco was founded in 1959. It has an enroll-ment of 190 students from nursery school (beginning at age two years, nine months) through twelfth grade. Average class size is 15. School hours are from 8:30 a.m. to 3:30 p.m. Extended day care is available until 5:45 p.m. Transporta-tion is provided. There is a dress code.

Registered with the State Department of Education.

•**Philosophy/Goals/Curriculum:** "The Hebrew Academy is a Jewish day school which gives an excellent college preparatory education in conjunction with a strong Jewish education. It is a warm and close environment where teachers and administration are involved with the students as individuals and provide educa-tion tailored to individual needs."

•**Admission Requirements and Procedure:** "Admission procedure is an initial meeting with the dean and vice principals (Judaic studies and secular studies) with entrance examination to determine if student is capable of maintaining grade-level work in both secular and Judaic studies. Admission is also dependent on available classroom space."

•**Most Recent Fee Schedule:** Nursery and Pre-kindergarten: $2,900 per year; Kindergarten: $3,300 per year; Grades one through eight: $3,900 per year; Grades nine through twelve: $4,300 per year. Day care is available for an additional fee. Scholarships are sometimes available; the scholarship committee meets as needed.

HERGL SCHOOL

1570 Greenwich Street (at Franklin), San Francisco, CA 94123

(415) 474-0191

•**Director:** Friederike Fearney

•**Assistant Director:** Sandra Wehrung

Hergl School was created in 1951. It is "a residential and day school specializing in the treatment of children whose primary diagnosis is mental retardation, chronic brain disorder, or psychotic disorder, including childhood autism and schizophrenia." Children and young adults ages four to twenty-one are served.

Hergl School has a capacity of ten students – five residential and five day. For the day students, school hours are from 8:30 a.m. to 3:30 p.m., with flexible day care hours. The program continues throughout the year. The school has a family life environment because the two directors of the program and their families live in the house.

Hergl School is licensed by the State Department of Health as a Group Home and Day Care Center for children and adults; by the State Department of Education as a NonPublic School (NPS); and vendorized by Golden Gate Regional Center.

•**Philosophy/Goals/Curriculum:** "To establish a relationship with the child by getting the child to leave his private, inner world and deal with the demands and consequences which the teacher presents; to involve the child in meaningful work; to overcome the negativism; to eliminate the most disturbing behaviors; to make the child a member of a group; to increase the child's desire and ability to communicate; to increase the ability of the child to care for his own personal needs; to increase the child's functional and intellectual skills to maximum potential."

•**Admission Requirements and Procedure:** The initial step is an interview with the parents and a medical report or examination. Multiple handicapped children, including hearing impaired and epileptic, are accepted. Children must be ambulatory and have no severe heart defects. The child applicant, usually between four and thirteen at admission age, is asked to participate in a three-month trial placement. Parent cooperation with the program is required.

•**Most Recent Fee Schedule:** Residential fee is set by Golden Gate Regional Center. The Day Program is $65.00 per day. Public School District funding through PL 94-142 is accepted. Private placement is available for either the Residential or Day Program.

HILLWOOD ACADEMIC DAY SCHOOL

2521 Scott Street (between Broadway and Pacific), San Francisco, CA 94115
(415) 931-0400

- •**Director:** Mary Libra
- •**Assistant Director:** Eric Grantz

Hillwood School was founded in 1949. It is a traditional independent, full-day school enrolling boys and girls in kindergarten through the eighth grade. It has a capacity of 125 students. Cow Hollow Kindergarten is the kindergarten department of Hillwood School. It provides full-day enrichment and an academic program using its own reading system developed over thirty-three years. Students arrive anytime between 7:30 a.m. and 9:00 a.m., and leave anytime between 3:00 pm. and 6:00 p.m. Program includes hot lunch, afternoon snacks, foreign language, art and choral music. There is an optional summer session during July. Uniforms are required.

Registered with the State Department of Education. Approved by the U.S. Department of State for foreign students.

- •**Philosophy/Goals/Curriculum:** "Hillwood follows the European Alpine tradition of thorough, basic academic instruction in a well-ordered, relaxed family atmosphere." The founder, Mary Libra, is still active in the school, assisted by staff and family member Eric Grantz. Hillwood considers it important that teachers and staff work closely to give each child a secure feeling of belonging to an understanding and caring family.
- •**Admission Requirements and Procedure:** Application for enrollment may be made at any time during the year by phoning for a half-hour school interview. There is a visiting and testing procedure if the school has space for the child.
- •**Most Recent Fee Schedule:** Tuition: $300 per month. Application Fee: $120. A number of scholarships are available after a student has attended Hillwood for one school year. For example, Hillwood Merit Scholarships are achieved by most students and are based on academic effort, achievement, and citizenship.

HOLY NAME OF JESUS SCHOOL

1560 40th Avenue (Lawton and 40th Avenue), San Francisco, CA 94122
(415) 731-4077

•**Principal:** Mrs. Noreen Murphy

Holy Name School has been in existence since 1940. It serves 514 pupils, kindergarten through eighth grade. Nineteen full-time and three part-time credentialed teachers are on staff. Average class size is 30. School hours are from 8:00 a.m. to 2:30 p.m. Extended day care is available until 6:00 p.m. Uniforms are required. There is a six week summer session/summer camp.

Accredited by WASC and WCEA.

•**Philosophy/Goals/Curriculum:** "The Christian Community is at the heart of Christian education. It is not a concept to be taught but a reality to be lived. As members of Holy Name School community, we have certain Religious Education Goals: That all members of the school community will grow in their knowledge and understanding of the teaching of the gospel; that the school community will grow into a faith community where Christian values are internalized and expressed in action; that the Holy Name School Community will be oriented toward service. We also have Intellectual Goals: That students will gain the cultural and intellectual values which foster a life-long love of learning; that students will gain the knowledge and skills necessary to be able to make informed decisions and to live meaningful and productive lives. Students and staff will grow in self understanding and self acceptance; each child will realize that Christ gives his people different gifts and each must serve the other for the good of all. . . . We aim to develop a program which encourages every student to work toward total well being. Students experience a wide range of teaching styles and methods in a well-rounded program and after school activities."

•**Admission Requirements and Procedure:** Kindergarten applicants are screened for readiness. Children must be five years old before December 1 of kindergarten year. All incoming students are tested, parents are interviewed, tour of school is given. Parents are notified of acceptance within a week of testing.

•**Most Recent Fee Schedule:** $140 - $160 per month for ten months; due the 15th of each month, August-May. Financial aid is available in the form of Archdiocesan family grant; Parish scholarship for Catholic students; school provides one year financial aid up to $4,500.

IMMACULATE CONCEPTION ACADEMY

3625 24th Street (at Guerrero), San Francisco, CA 94110
(415) 824-2052

•**Principal:** Sister Jonelle Martin Fixa, O.P.

Immaculate Conception Academy was founded in 1883. It has an enrollment of 300 girls, grades nine through twelve. Average class size is 22, with 21 teachers on the staff. School hours are from 7:45 a.m. to 2:45 p.m. with an optional early-bird class. Uniforms are required. Accredited by WASC.

•**Philosophy/Goals/Curriculum:** "Built on the traditions of academic excellence and a warm, family atmosphere, the Academy encourages its students to develop fully their intellectual gifts, to build a life-long set of Christian values and to participate in curricular and co-curricular activities, thereby fostering their development as well-rounded individuals. A solid foundation in liberal arts is part of the college preparatory and business education programs. Students have the option of combining these."

•**Admission Requirements and Procedure:** "Initial interview with parents and students by ICA faculty (December); average or above-average scoring on placement test (January) and seventh and eighth grade scholastic averages; recommendation of principal and/or eighth-grade teacher concerning the student's character and academic achievement and potential (February). A genuine interest shown by the student and her parents in cooperating with school philosophy and policies. Notification is in the first week in March."

•**Most Recent Fee Schedule:** Tuition: $2,800 per year, plus $325 registration and fees. Partial scholarships are available to students and families based on need and merit. $80,000 total was awarded during 1988-89 for scholarships.

INTERNATIONAL CHRISTIAN SCHOOL

42 Waller Street (near Octavia and Market), San Francisco, CA 94102
(415) 863-1691

•**Principal:** Obadiah Patnaik

The International Christian School of the First Baptist Church, founded in 1971, is truly international and multi-ethnic. Seventeen countries are represented by its students, ranging from two years of age through seventh graders. Total enrollment is 325 with expansion anticipated. The nineteen teachers are credentialed. Average class size is 15 for preschool and 20 for grade school. The preschool program consists of four classes: nursery — two year olds; prekindergarten — three year olds; kindergarten — four year olds; senior kindergarten — five year olds. Each teacher has an aide. Speech screening is available once a year. School hours are from 8:30 a.m. to 3:00 p.m.; the extended day care program is from 7:00 a.m. to 6:00 p.m. It is a year-round program with a reduced size summer school.

Registered with the State Department of Education and accredited by the Association of Christian Schools International.

•**Philosophy/Goals/Curriculum:** "The primary purpose of the School is to provide opportunity for children on the Primary and Elementary level in a Christ-centered academic environment. Academic subjects (literature, sciences, social sciences) are presented in Christian perspective. Mental objectives of the school are to equip the child with the fundamental tools of learning, with the knowledge, skills, attitudes, appreciation and pre-dispositions that are commensurate with the child's ability and grade placement. Wholesome social experiences are provided by means of the classroom and playground. The school dedicates itself to academic excellence and spiritual sensitivities. Early American concepts of God, home, country and authority are emphasized. The school helps its students acquire independence, self-reliance, emotional stability, self-discipline and self-confidence."

•**Admission Requirements and Procedure:** Open to all children on a space available basis. Kindergarteners through seventh graders are tested during the summer to determine placement for admission. Other criteria for admission include test scores, grades, and conduct reports.

•**Most Recent Fee Schedule:** Tuition: $165 per month; extended day care: $80 per month. Registration fee: $70.

JAMESTOWN LEARNING CENTER

25 14th Street (Harrison), San Francisco, CA 94103
(415) 863-2611

•**Director:** Peter Zabriskie

Jamestown Learning Center was established in 1979 to serve children and adolescents with learning disabilities, behavior problems, and/or in crisis. The age range of students is from twelve to twenty-one. The school's capacity is 30, with an enrollment of 24. There are eight teachers and a speech and language therapist. The staff is involved in a continuous, rigorous in-service training program. Average class size is eight. School hours are from 8:30 a.m. to 1:00 p.m. After school activities include outdoor education and adventure, vocational education, and computer training. A summer school program is provided. Limited transportation services available.

Registered with the State Department of Education.

•**Philosophy/Goals/Curriculum:** Jamestown Learning Center is "an alternative school for youth who have failed in the public school system. One major goal is to return the youth to the public school system. Methods of approach include use of precision learning concepts along with a token economy system, goal contracting, and use of communication and problem solving skills based on an effectiveness training model. The program includes basic academic subjects with credits applied toward a high school diploma. The program also provides vocational training; basic skills training; employment services; individual and family counseling; and a physical education program that includes swimming, exercise, and weight lifting. Vocational-educational skills are emphasized. Students are provided the opportunity to learn various clerical skills and the use of business machines. The focus is on assessment and goal setting."

•**Admission Requirements and Procedure:** Students are admitted in consultation with the placement service of the Public School System.

•**Most Recent Fee Schedule:** Funding is provided by the local school districts. Scholarships are provided for exceptional students who don't qualify under P.L. 94-142.

KATHERINE DELMAR BURKE SCHOOL

7070 California Street (at 32nd Avenue), San Francisco, CA 94121
(415) 751-0177

•**Headmaster:** David Fleishhacker

The Katherine Delmar Burke School offers an advanced and challenging course of study for girls from kindergarten through grade eight. The school was founded in 1908 and moved to its present location in 1975. A 203-acre outdoor education center was added in 1987. The school has an enrollment of 360 girls; the maximum class size is 22. There are 38 teachers on staff. An extended care program for children in kindergarten through fourth grade is available. Lunches may be purchased at the school. There are summer programs on campus and at the school's outdoor campus. Uniforms are required. Accredited by CAIS.

•**Philosophy/Goals/Curriculum:** "The school's purpose is to provide an exceptional education for girls of ability and motivation. Thus its curriculum is demanding and its program designed to promote academic achievement and the development of the individual. The program is designed as a continuum. The goal is a graduating eighth grader confident of her ability to achieve at a superior academic level."

•**Admission Requirements and Procedure:** The school's admissions committee selects students who are likely to succeed in a challenging program. At the kindergarten level, individual evaluations and observations by the faculty, administration, and educational psychologists are used. In later grades, academic potential, leadership, character, and other factors are weighed against the needs of the class to be entered.

•**Most Recent Fee Schedule:** Tuition ranges from $4,900 for kindergarten to $5,800 for eighth grade per year. The activity fee ranges from $100 to $200 per year depending upon grade level. Additional costs are optional lunches, uniforms, materials fees for special classes in the upper grades, and the school yearbook. A large scholarship program is available.

KATHERINE MICHIELS SCHOOL

1335 Guerrero Street (between 25th and 26th streets), San Francisco, CA 94110
(415) 821-1434

•**Owner:** Katherine Michiels

Katherine Michiels School was founded in 1984. It has an enrollment of 80 students with ages from three months through second graders. All KMS staff are experienced early childhood education specialists. The teacher - child ratio is 1:4 for infants; 1:8 for preschoolers; and 1:15 for elementary grades. School hours are from 6:30 a.m. to 6:30 p.m. Extended care is available until 12:00 midnight.

•**Philosophy/Goals/Curriculum:** "Katherine Michiels School provides a well-balanced program of academic education, creative shared play and structured activities that include verbal skills, initiative ability and individual self-confidence to insure an active school experience for children as they grow up. . . . The staff recognizes the need to teach children necessary discipline and realistic limits, so that they develop the tools to make active choices which have consequences that result in responsible behavior. Day care is a choice you make for your child so he or she can achieve his or her maximum potential. Teachers, caretakers and parents must work together to give examples and create a harmony of influences, disciplines, values and problem-solving techniques to guide your child through his or her most valuable years."

•**Admission Requirements and Procedure:** All applications are welcome. Admission is by interview acceptance, space availability and completion of enrollment application.

•**Most Recent Fee Schedule:** Ages four and three-quarters to eight: $385 per month for full time (five day week); Ages two and one-half to four and three-quarters: $450 per month for full time (five day week); Ages three months to two and one-half: $575 per month for full time (five day week).

Evening Care: minimum of three full days per week: $3 - $4 hourly rate.

After School: $2 - $3 hourly rate. $40 enrollment fee.

KITTREDGE SCHOOL

2355 Lake Street (at 25th Avenue), San Francisco, CA 94121
(415) 751-3050

•**Principal:** Shirley Freeman

Kittredge School was established in 1944. It currently has 103 students enrolled in grades one through eight. The teacher-student ratio is 1:15. All teachers are credentialed. School hours are from 8:40 a.m. to 3:00 p.m. Extended day care is available from 7:30 a.m. to 6:00 p.m. A summer school program, academic in the morning with enrichment activities in the afternoon, is open to students from other schools. The school accepts a few students with learning difficulties, but parents must arrange for outside remedial services. A comprehensive literature-based reading program is stressed. An after school academy provides enrichment activities for all qualified elementary and junior high students in San Francisco.

Registered with the State Department of Education and accredited by NAIS.

•**Philosophy/Goals/Curriculum:** "Kittredge School is committed to providing for its students a strong academic program within a nurturing atmosphere. The curriculum is designed to prepare students for an academic high school experience. A strong emphasis is placed on communication between the school and home. Through the small classes, faculty members are able to individualize the academic program when appropriate. Further, Kittredge School recognizes the need for creative expression and an introduction to the fine arts and a foreign language. All students are enrolled in a French program and a computer literacy program. The school provides a formal Physical Education program of a minimum four days per week. . . . Skills in individual and team sports are emphasized as are the qualities of sportsmanship and fair play. Kittredge School is structured, friendly and productive. We believe in recognizing the worth and dignity of students and faculty alike and in creating an atmosphere of strong academic goals combined with supportive human contact."

•**Admission Requirements and Procedure:** There is a parent and student interview. The child is invited to spend time at the school. Testing and evaluation are used to help determine eligibility. April 1 is the deadline for deposit for the following fall. Students are accepted from the waiting list if a mid-year opening occurs.

•**Most Recent Fee Schedule:** Tuition for grades one through four: $4,200 per year; Tuition for grades five through eight: $4,400 per year; Registration fee: $100.

LAKESIDE PRESBYTERIAN CENTER FOR CHILDREN

201 Eucalyptus Drive (at 19th Avenue), San Francisco, CA 94132
(415) 564-5044

•**Director:** Louanne Heath

Lakeside was founded in 1959 and accepts children two and one-half to six years of age. Current enrollment is 140 children, with four credentialed teachers, 19 aides, and one music specialist. Nursery school and kindergarten classes are offered, as well as day care from 7:30 a.m. to 6:00 p.m. Children attending other nursery schools or kindergartens will be accepted at 12:00 p.m. No drop-in day care is available. Parents must attend one nightly meeting per month, work in the child's classroom twice each month, and actively participate 30 hours per academic year.

Licensed by the State Department of Social Services and Accredited by the National Academy of Early Childhood Programs.

•**Philosophy/Goals/Curriculum:** "It is our purpose to extend Christian Education early into the lives of young children to help guide them in all aspects of growth and at the same time provide parents with a program of education and care that is nurturing in atmosphere and Christian in spirit and orientation. The purpose can only be achieved through total involvement of the parents and the church."

•**Admission Requirements and Procedure:** First come, first served.

•**Most Recent Fee Schedule:** Two days per week: $75 per month; three days per week: $113 per month; five days per week: $188 per month; full time day care with nursery school/kindergarten: $402 per month; part-time day care: $2.89 per hour. Scholarships are available. Active, pledging members of Lakeside Presbyterian Church eligible for a 15 percent discount.

LA MEL SCHOOL

1801 Bush Street (at Octavia), San Francisco, CA 94109
(415) 931-1972

•**Director:** LaVonne Lomba
•**Administrator:** Ms. Melanie Lomba Howard

La Mel School was founded in 1970. It is "a day treatment facility for children and adolescents who, because of emotional or neurological handicaps, manifest adjustment problems at home, at school, or in the community." The capacity of La Mel is 75 students, ages four to twenty-one. Students work in groups of six to eight. The multidisciplinary staff of 37 includes Ryan credentialed teachers; physicians; psychologists; art, movement and sensory motor and learning specialists; occupational therapists, social workers and speech therapists. School hours are from 9:30 a.m. to 2:30 p.m. A summer school program is provided.

Registered with the State Department of Education as a Non-Public School (NPS); the school can grant high school diplomas; also registered by the Joint Commission on Accreditation of Hospitals as a Partial Day Hospital.

•**Philosophy/Goals/Curriculum:** La Mel provides services for children with average intelligence or above, who manifest social, emotional, learning, and behavioral problems. Each child is assessed initially. A total treatment program is designed with the family and child. Progress is reviewed weekly and plans are updated at regular intervals. La Mel aims to "cultivate academic potential, foster social maturity, develop life management skills and further physical maturity." The goal is to get the student back into the mainstream. For students over fourteen years of age, vocational testing and training are provided as well as work placement. For graduating seniors, college testing, placement, and field trips are also part of the program.

•**Admission Requirements and Procedure:** La Mel has a multidisciplinary intake procedure. "Children who are four to twenty-one years of age, who are of at least average intelligence, and who possess sufficient personal strengths to make significant progress in the program are accepted." Parent participation is mandatory.

•**Most Recent Fee Schedule:** 1) Tuition determined by individual school boards. 2) Special education evaluation fee/aid available. 3) Medical fees determined by California Relative Value Studies (CRVS) and set by individual physicians.

THE LAUREL SCHOOL

350 9th Avenue (between Geary and Clement streets), San Francisco, CA 94118 (415) 752-3567

•**Director of Admissions:** Joyce Witkowski
•**Headmistress:** Marcia Spitz
The Laurel School, established in 1964, is a private academic school for preschool through ninth grade. School capacity is 100 students. The teacher-student ratio is 1:10. School hours are from 8:45 a.m. to 3:00 p.m. Pre-kindergarten full day: 8:45 a.m. to 3:00 p.m.; half day: 8:45 a.m. to 12:00 p.m. Extended day care and summer school programs are also available. The school program is departmentalized, and the curriculum includes foreign languages, computers, and drama. The staff members hold California credentials while some also hold learning specialist credentials. The Laurel High School was established in 1985 in response to a need for a high school in San Francisco that provided a rigorous college preparatory curriculum for students who need a small classroom setting.
Registered with the State Department of Education.
•**Philosophy/Goals/Curriculum:** "The Laurel School offers an opportunity for academic success in a small classroom setting. Students gain self-confidence in a

warm and loving atmosphere where achievement is carefully evaluated."

•**Admission Requirements and Procedure:** Parent and student interview, testing for admission/placement, and recommendation from former school.

•**Most Recent Fee Schedule:** Tuition: $6,000 per year. Prekindergarten: $3,000 for half day; $5,000 for full day. Sibling Discount: 10 - 25%. Scholarships available.

LICK-WILMERDING HIGH SCHOOL

755 Ocean Avenue (at I-280), San Francisco, CA 94112
(415) 333-4021

•**Headmaster:** Albert M. Adams, Ed.D.

Lick-Wilmerding is a coeducational, independent secondary high school founded in 1885. Present enrollment totals 330 students in grades nine through twelve. The school's rigorous college-preparatory academic program is complimented by rich offerings in the technical arts, visual and performing arts, and athletics. Due to its endowment and financial aid commitment, Lick enjoys an exceptionally diverse student body. The average class size is 14. School hours are 8:00 a.m. to 3:00 p.m.

Accredited by WASC. Member NAIS and CAIS.

•**Philosophy/Goals/Curriculum:** "Lick-Wilmerding is a college preparatory high school whose purpose is to help academically able students develop qualities of the head, heart and hands which will serve them well in college and life. The School's goal is to produce self-directed, lifelong learners who approach the world with sensitivity, creativity, competence, compassion and a can-do confidence."

•**Admission Requirements and Procedure:** Prospective students submit written applications by January 26, accompanying essays, transcripts, and evaluations from former schools, and a parent's form. Either the SSAT or the ERB examination is required, as is a student visit and interview. Notification of acceptance is March 16.

•**Most Recent Fee Schedule:** Tuition: $6,250 per year. Twenty-five percent of Lick's students are financially aided.

LIVE OAK SCHOOL

117 Diamond Street (at 18th Street), San Francisco, CA 94114

(415) 861-8840

•**Director:** Lee A. Turner-Muecke

Live Oak School was founded in 1971. It has an enrollment of 105 students, from kindergarten through grade six. Teacher-student ratio is 1:15 and teachers are credentialed. School hours are 9:00 a.m. to 3:00 p.m., except on Wednesdays, 9:00 a.m. to 2:00 p.m. Extended day care is available from 7:30 a.m. to 9:00 a.m. and from 3:00 p.m. to 6:00 p.m. A summer school progam is provided.

Registered with the State Department of Education.

•**Philosophy/Goals/Curriculum:** "Live Oak School was founded by parents and teachers seeking to provide a progressive educational environment for young children. From the beginning Live Oak School was concerned with the physical, social, emotional and academic development of each child. Believing that schools represent an extension of the environment and experience of the family, Live Oak began with a commitment to parent participation. Our purpose is to: Help children fully develop their academic skills and interests; assist children in the natural development of their curiosity and love of learning; allow children to develop self-confidence, self-respect and independence; and develop in children a cooperative attitude and an ability to act out of concern and compassion for others. A strong intergenerational program is in effect at Live Oak School."

•**Admission Requirements and Procedure:** "Considerations for admission include the compatibility of the educational philosophy of the parents and the school, the student's ability to benefit from the program, and the desire of the parents to be involved in their child's education. The school's program is not suited to children with severe emotional or academic problems."

•**Most Recent Fee Schedule:** Tuition is $3,475 per year. A sibling reduction is given to parents with more than one child in the school. In addition to tuition, there is a work assessment which is refundable after 60 hours of parent participation. Daycare costs are separate from tuition, and must be paid in advance. Tuition aid is available to families with financial need.

LYCEE FRANCAIS FRENCH SCHOOL

3301 Balboa Street (at 34th Avenue), San Francisco, CA 94121
(415) 668-1833

•**Principal:** Pierre Hudelot
•**Director of Admissions:** Elizabeth Hughes
   The French Lycee was founded in 1967 by a group of French and French-speaking parents. They wanted to find the means to preserve or regain their original language and culture for their children. The enrollment is 275 students from pre-kindergarten through twelfth grade, on two campuses. Kindergarten and elementary classes are at 834 28th Avenue; sixth through twelfth grades are at 3301 Balboa Street. Class size is limited to 22 students. Teachers are credentialed in France, except for the English teachers, who are U.S. credentialed. Most teaching is in French except the English language and literature and American history courses. An American counselor is employed at the secondary level. School hours are from 8:30 a.m. to 3:15 p.m. or 4:00 p.m. for high school students. Day care is available until 6:00 p.m. Special English and French lessons are conducted for students who need individual support.
   Registered with the State Department of Education and accredited by the French government.
•**Philosophy/Goals/Curriculum:** "The Lycee Francais French School combines a French-American education for students from three years to eighteen years, according to the standards of the French Ministry of Education. (The French government provides some funding for the school.) The preschool and kindergarten are language immersion programs that prepare children for the elementary school which is a structured, very academic program. It prepares students for the "French Baccalaureat" which gives access to both American and European universities. In American universities, the French Baccalaureat is equivalent to a year of university-level study. There are four kinds of Baccalaureat: mathematics, literature, science, and economics. Everyone must study French literature, history, geography, science, physics, economics, American history, philosophy, mathematics, and Spanish (after the sixth grade). Extra-curricular activities include sports, theatre, music, computers, and electronics."
•**Admission Requirements and Procedure:** The Lycee Francais accepts everyone. It prefers to get children by kindergarten, and children entering after grade

two must have prior knowledge of French.

•**Most Recent Fee Schedule:** Registration fee: $200 per family (once only); Application fee: $100 (credited toward tuition); Kindergarten through twelfth grade: $4,250 - $6,000 depending on grade. French government and school scholarships available.

MARIA MONTESSORI SCHOOL OF THE GOLDEN GATE

678 Portola Drive (at Woodside), San Francisco, CA 94127

(415) 731-8188

•**Headmistress:** Ursula Thrush

The Maria Montessori School of the Golden Gate was founded in 1972. It accepts children from eighteen months to twelve years. The teacher-student ratio is 1:10. The teachers on the staff are credentialed and/or Montessori trained. Handicapped children are accepted. School hours are from 9:00 a.m. to 3:00 p.m. Summer camp is provided.

Registered with the State Department of Education.

•**Philosophy/Goals/Curriculum:** "The Junior school is the time and place for Cosmic Education. The children are in two groups: six to nine-year-olds and nine to twelve-year-olds. The six to nine-year-olds perfect their intellectual tools of reading, writing, mathematics, and learn to use their time constructively by finishing projects started. The nine to twelve-year-olds may then embark on individual research. We prepare an environment into which we channel activities and experiences pertaining to the formation of the Earth, and the evolution of life and consciousness on this planet from the first unicellular beings to man and his achievements. This large vision stimulates the child into the study of his own particular field of interest only to discover that his field is interrelated and interdependent with every other field in life."

•**Admission Requirements and Procedure:** Children are accepted on a space available basis. The parent submits an enrollment application with a non-refundable application fee of $25.

•**Most Recent Fee Schedule:** Tuition: $3,400 per year. Extended hour care varies according to the number of hours.

MERCY HIGH SCHOOL

3250 19th Avenue (between Winston and Eucalyptus), San Francisco, CA 94132
(415) 334-0525

•**Principal:** James H. Ernst

   Mercy High School was founded in 1953 and has an enrollment of 600 girls, grades nine through twelve. Average class size is 25, with 35 full-time and six part-time teachers, all credentialed by the State of California. School hours are 8:00 a.m. to 3:00 p.m. Uniforms are required. A summer school program is provided.

   Accredited by WASC and WCEA.

•**Philosophy/Goals/Curriculum:** "Mercy High School is a four-year college preparatory high school, owned and sponsored by the Sisters of Mercy. Mercy provides an educational environment in which students grow and develop in a wide variety of expeiences. We encourage intellectual integrity, aesthetic sensitivity, responsible decision making, warm, open relationships, and maturing faith in Christ. Our college curriculum is rich and varied – our many honors and Advanced Placement courses challenge the most able students; most of our classes provide excellent educational opportunities for the above average student. Mercy also offers a curriculum for those students who need additional assistance with their studies." Many fine arts and business courses are also in the curriculum.

•**Admission Requirements and Procedure:** A student must be able to work well in a college preparatory environment. Prospective students should call or write the admissions office for catalogues and applications. Most applications are processed in the spring; Mercy does accept qualified students year round.

•**Most Recent Fee Schedule:** Tuition: $3,450 per year; registration fee: $200; book rental fee: $85. Financial aid is available.

MONTESSORI HOUSE OF CHILDREN

1187 Franklin Street (entrance on Geary), San Francisco, CA 94109
(415) 441-7691

•**Adminstrator:** Roland Wanigatunga
•**Director:** Amala Wijesinghe

   The Montessori House of Children was founded in 1976. It has an enrollment of 100 students from two and one-half to eight years old. Average class size is 24, with a teacher and a teacher's assistant. The teachers all have Montessori diplomas, and the assistants are college graduates. Regular school hours are from 9:00 a.m. to 3:00 p.m. with extended day care available from 7:00 a.m. to 9:00 a.m. and 3:00 p.m. to 6:00 p.m. The school provides a year-round program, with one week's vacation in April and July, at which times day care is available. The school is closed for a twelve day winter vacation in December.

Registered with the State Department of Education.

•**Philosophy/Goals/Curriculum:** "Montessori House of Children is based on the philosophy of Dr. Maria Montessori. It provides what Dr. Montessori called 'freedom within limits.' The environment is prepared with activities in practical life, sensorial, language, and math, supplemented with art, movement, science, history, and geography. It is equipped with specially designed Montessori apparatus from Holland, and additional activities prepared by the directresses. Children are encouraged in the development of self-discipline, self-knowledge, independence, enthusiasm for learning, an organized approach to problem solving, and academic skills; they are also exposed to art, cultural subjects, French, movement and dance, yoga, piano, and computer."

•**Admission Requirements and Procedure:** Children are accepted on a space-available basis.

•**Most Recent Fee Schedule:** Registration fee (non-refundable): $40; tuition deposit: one month's tuition; total tuition for children ages two and one-half to four: $300 per month.

MORRISANIA WEST INC.
SAN FRANCISCO POSTAL STREET ACADEMY

914 Divisadero Street (between McAllister and Eddy), San Francisco, CA 94115
(415) 563-7934

•**Principal:** Peter LeDuff

The Postal Street Academy is part of Morrisania West Inc., a Youth Diversion Program. It emerged from the National Postal Academy when San Francisco was designated as one of the six cities to implement the Postal Street Academy in 1970. Its present enrollment is 44 youths, aged 14 through 18. Maximum class size is 13 students. There are four credentialed teachers, two private and two from

S.F. Unified School District. The program serves the needs of teenagers who have been truant, expelled from school, runaways, or out of parental control. Morrisania West, Inc., Postal Street Academy offers legal, medical, and emergency shelter services in addition to the educational program. A summer school program is provided. This Youth Diversion Program is sponsored by the Mayor's Criminal Justice Council.

•**Philosophy/Goals/Curriculum:** "The ultimate goal of the Postal Street Academy Youth Diversion Program 'is to divert youths from the criminal justice system and to recycle youths back into schools and mainstream of the community.' This is an alternative education program that provides intensive individual and group tutoring and counseling. Visual arts training, job development, and field trips are also included. The Academy has been successful in motivating numerous students to higher education, working closely with the Board of Education to help return students to the public school system, graduating youths who were once considered high school problems, and cutting the recidivism rate to less than three percent."

•**Admission Requirements and Procedure:** The program is designed to work in a complementary manner with the following agencies: The San Francisco Unified School District; The Youth Guidance Center; The Department of Social Services; The Police Department. Interested youth seeking help may self-refer.

•**Funding:** Provided by the Mayor's Criminal Justice Council and by private contributions.

MOTHER GOOSE SCHOOL INC.

334 28th Avenue (between California and Clement), San Francisco, CA 94121
(415) 221-6133

•**Headmaster:** Dana Hemberger

Mother Goose School was established in 1951 and has a current enrollment of 110 students, ages two to seven. The school offers nursery school through second grade classes. A hot lunch and two snacks are served. The school is open from 7:00 a.m. to 6:00 p.m. Children may attend on a full-time or part-time schedule. Mother Goose School is open eleven and a half months a year.

Licensed by the State Department of Health. Charter Member of Private Nursery School Association (PACE).

•**Philosophy/Goals/Curriculum:** "Mother Goose School offers a well-rounded program for all children at all levels and stages of development. Instruction is individualized and all-inclusive to give the children a firm foundation in preparation for private schools in the Bay Area. The daily program includes activities which reflect our dedication to the development of the mind, body and character of the young child. Academics, the arts, music, physical education and social interaction are a part of every school day. In the nursery we offer toilet training for the untrained child and a nap for those on full-time schedules. Our main emphasis is towards the development of a positive self-concept in each child and an enjoyment of learning that will continue throughout life."

•**Admission Requirements and Procedure:** A parent-child interview at the school.

•**Most Recent Fee Schedule:** Registration and insurance: $250; Full-time (including lunch): $525 per month; Part-time with lunch: $375 per month; Part-time without lunch: $325 per month; Toilet training: $50 per month.

NEW LEARNING SCHOOL
1016 Eddy (near Gough), San Francisco, CA 94109
(415) 923-9900

•**Director:** Terrence Clancy

The New Learning School (formerly the Independent Learning School) is a sixth to twelfth grade private, non-profit school providing one-on-one instruction and customized learning plans for students in standard and college preparatory programs. We maintain a 12:1 student - teacher ratio and focus on the individual. A second campus of the New Learning School is located in Berkeley.

Accredited by WASC.

•**Philosophy/Goals/Curriculum:** "We believe a school should prepare a student to learn academic material thoroughly, progress rapidly, and prepare to meet the challenges of higher education or the working world. Each student works in academic areas appropriate to his academic needs. He must pass each assignment at the 90 percent or above level. This assures the student of a thorough understanding of each subject in his academic program before going on to the next assignment. If a student scores less than 90 percent, he receives timely tutorial help and is tested once again to demonstrate mastery."

•**Admission Requirements and Procedure:** Enrollment is continuous throughout the year. Students are requested to visit the school. Achievement tests in reading, writing, mathematics, and language are administered to determine areas in which the student excels or needs help, and to measure the school's teaching effectiveness with the student.

•**Most Recent Fee Schedule:** Tuition: $6,100 per year; Summer school: $95.00 per week. Scholarships are available.

OAKES CHILDREN'S CENTER

1348 10th Avenue (between Irving and Judah), San Francisco, CA 94122
(415) 564-2310

•**Director:** Rob Tyminski

Oakes Children's Center was established in 1963 in a landmark fire house built in 1899. Twenty children are currently enrolled, ages four to thirteen. The program is ungraded and designed to meet the needs of severely emotionally disturbed children and their families. The teacher-student ratio is 3:5. Teachers have special education credentials. The school is open eleven months a year, and school hours are from 9:00 a.m. to 2:00 p.m., Monday through Thursday; 9:00 a.m. to 1:00 p.m., Fridays. Transportation is provided. A summer school program is available.

Registered with the State Department of Education as a Non-Public School.

•**Philosophy/Goals/Curriculum:** Oakes Center strives to "provide a therapeutic-educational program for both severely disturbed children and their families with the goal of optimally developing whatever potential the child has available so his growth can proceed along normal developmental lines. It is hoped that: a) each youngster will be less of a disruptive influence within the home and that parents, siblings, relatives and friends can understand and enjoy the youngster to a greater extent than was true prior to enrollment; b) children may make adjustments to public school; c) parents may experience greater confidence and comfort in their role as parents; d) parents can comfortably consider residential placement if this is in the child's best interests." There is a comprehensive clinical program under the supervision of a psychiatrist, psychologist, and clinical social worker.

•**Admission Requirements and Procedure:** Referrals are made by the Placement Office of the San Francisco Unified School District.

•**Most Recent Fee Schedule:** No cost to parents. Funding is through PL 94-142,

State Law 3632, and Short-Doyle.

ONE FIFTY PARKER STREET SCHOOL

150 Parker Street (between Geary and Euclid), San Francisco, CA 94118
(415) 221-0294

•**Director:** Doris M. Welsh

One Fifty Parker Street School was organized in 1954 to provide for a full range of children's interests and abilities. There are currently 60 children, ages two and three-quarters to six, enrolled in the program. Nursery School hours are from 9:00 a.m. to 12:00 p.m. and from 1:00 p.m. to 4:00 p.m. Kindergarten is from 8:15 a.m. to 12:15 p.m. Child care is available from 8:00 a.m. to 9:00 a.m., lunch hour, and from 4:00p.m. to 6:00 p.m. There is a summer program available for children two and one-half to six years old.

Licensed by the State Department of Social Services.

•**Philosophy/Goals/Curriculum:** "A multi-disciplinary, developmentally based approach is utilized to encourage children to grow and develop in all areas – cognitive, social, emotional, and motor. There are no entrance tests or screenings, and a limited number of handicapped children are welcome. There is a great deal of parent involvement and cooperation, but the program is the responsibility of the professional staff."

•**Admission Requirements and Procedure:** Visitation followed by application and placement on the waiting list.

•**Most Recent Fee Schedule:** Nursery School: $2,188 per academic year (ten months); Kindergarten: $2,318 per academic year; Child Care, noon to 5:30: $2,292 per ten months; or $2.25 per hour. Some limited scholarships are available.

THE OPEN BOOK SCHOOL

2031 Bush Street (between Buchanan and Webster), San Francisco, CA 94115
(415) 563-6732

•**Principal:** David Whitmore

The Open Book School opened in 1981. It is an ungraded elementary school for learning disabled children from eight to thirteen years old. School capacity is

12 to 18 students in three classrooms. Teachers are credentialed and experienced in teaching children with a variety of learning styles. School hours are from 9:00 a.m. to 3:00 p.m. Summer school is from 9:00 a.m. to 1:00 p.m.

Certified by the State of California as a special education school.

•**Philosophy/Goals/Curriculum:** The goals of the Open Book School are threefold: "To improve students' basic skills (reading, language arts, math); to further students' overall education (science, social studies, music, art); to develop students' independence (self-management; social and survival skills)." The School's program emphasizes the following: "Diagnosis and remediation of students' weaknesses; recognition and reinforcement of students' strengths; utilization of students' individual learning style; and multisensory instruction appealing to visual, auditory and kinesthetic learners." Learning activities are teacher-directed and individualized. "Behavior management techniques are humanistic and language-based, and include group process and one-to-one counseling in a therapeutic milieu which stresses personal responsibility and logical consequences, and concepts of community."

•**Admission Requirements and Procedure:** The parent and child are invited to come in for an interview. Previous school records are requested. The child is asked to do a variety of paper/pencil tasks. If placement in the School seems appropriate, the child spends one day in the classroom on a trial basis.

•**Most Recent Fee Schedule:** Children are funded by the San Francisco Unified School District under PL 94-142. Private placements are by arrangement with the parents and depend upon the child's needs and program.

PACIFIC PRIMARY SCHOOL

1500 Grove Street (at Baker), San Francisco, CA 94117
(415) 346-0906

•**Director:** Charlotte Burchard

Pacific Primary was founded in 1974 and currently has an enrollment of 81 children from two and one-half to six years of age. It has a nursery school and a kindergarten program. Extended day care is available. Breakfast, lunch, and a snack are served. The school is open from 7:00 a.m. to 6:30 p.m., twelve months a year. Limited parent participation is required.

Licensed by the State Department of Social Services.

•**Philosophy/Goals/Curriculum:** "Pacific Primary believes that the family bears the major responsibility for a child's learning and that the curriculum of the school should grow from mutual involvement of teachers, parents and students. Education, we believe, must prepare people to live a life – a creative, loving and humane life. The school offers a supportive environment where children will learn at their own pace, in ways that are meaningful to them, and develop the basic skills they need to realize their potential as unique human beings. The school emphasizes the interrelations of creative arts activities and academic learning in the young child."

•**Admission Requirements and Procedure:** Admission procedures consist of filing an application form, payment of an application fee, parent orientation meeting, and personal interview of child and parent with the Director to determine the child's readiness for the school program. There is no preadmission testing.

•**Most Recent Fee Schedule:** Registration fee: $25. Attendance 9:00 a.m. to 3:00 p.m.: $5,480 per year (12 months); 7 a.m. to 6:30 p.m.: $5,940 per year. A limited amount of scholarship aid is available.

THE PHOENIX ACADEMY

44 Page Street (between Gough and Franklin streets), San Francisco, CA 94102 (415) 554-0307

•**Principal:** Linda L. Chiarucci

The Phoenix Academy was established as Sunset Community School in 1970 and has an enrollment of 50 students from pre-kindergarten through twelfth grade. Average grouping is 15 students. School hours are from 8:30 a.m. to 2:30 p.m. Extended care is available. A day camp or tutoring is available during the summer.

Registered with the State Department of Education.

•**Philosophy/Goals/Curriculum:** "The common complaint we hear from a prospective parent is that his/her child is simply not motivated and not working to his/her potential. This is frequently the situation when a child is in a classroom with thirty to forty others. The goal of grade-level achievement for an entire class is an arduous task for any teacher, especially when many students endure a poor background in phonics, comprehension and basic math computation.

"The Phoenix Academy never 'labels' these students. They are simply unmotivated. In small student/teacher groupings, we choose to assign work that *any* student can handle comfortably, building a student's confidence. Our aim is that each student experience a sense of genuinely significant accomplishment, regardless of whether s/he is working on material that is above, below, or at the student's chronological grade level. Via monthly progress reports or quarter report cards, parent and student are aware of a student's achievement and attitude. In many instances, parent and teacher converse on a daily basis to check on homework or other study assignments. The consistency of such reports is often required to insure that a student works to his/her capacity. Thereby, children and parents alike can enjoy and benefit from the extended-family atmosphere of the school to strengthen the family unit and their children's academic progress."

•**Admission Requirements and Procedure:** Interview, completed application form and placement screening are required.

•**Most Recent Fee Schedule:** Tuition ranges from $2,500 per year for pre-kindergarten to $2,850 per year for grades six through twelve. Financial aid is available.

PRESENTATION HIGH SCHOOL

2350 Turk Street (at Masonic), San Francisco, CA 94118
(415) 387-4720

•**Principal:** Miss Anne Bellan

Presentation High School was established in 1854 and has an enrollment of 305 girls in grades nine through twelve. The average class size is 26. The 39 staff members are either credentialed or have advanced degrees. School hours are from 8:30 a.m. to 2:40 p.m. Uniforms are required.

Accredited by WASC.

•**Philosophy/Goals/Curriculum:** "Presentation High School strives to present the Christian faith as preserved and taught by the Catholic Church and to provide opportunities for the student to experience and grow in that faith; to engage each student in a curriculum which seeks to develop her whole being: her religious, intellectual, volitional, aesthetic, and physical powers; to offer the student an elective program broad enough for her to explore her interests and talents, and to prepare her according to her personal aspirations and aptitudes for higher education and/or profitable employment.

"The required sequence of four years each of Religion, English, and social science aims to prepare each student to assume her responsibility as a Christian woman in society. Also required for graduation are two years of mathematics and one year each of science, foreign language, creative arts and physical education."

•**Admission Requirements and Procedure:** The application process at Presentation High School includes a transcript from the applicant's elementary school with recommendations as to the prospective applicant's seriousness of purpose in continuing a Catholic education; a placement test; and a personal interview with the girl and her parents.

•**Most Recent Fee Schedule:** Application Fee: $30; Tuition: $3,350 per year, payable in 10 installments of $335; Registration fee: $150. Family rate and limited financial assistance are available.

PRESIDIO HILL SCHOOL

3839 Washington Street (between Maple and Cherry), San Francisco, CA 94118
(415) 751-9318

•**Principal:** Susan Andrews

Presidio Hill was founded in 1918 and currently enrolls 90 students in kindergarten through eighth grade. Class size is 15 to 18 students. All teachers are credentialed. Day care is available before school at 8:00 a.m. and after school until 6:00 p.m. Field trips and outdoor education are an integral part of the program.

Registered with the State Department of Education.

•**Philosophy/Goals/Curriculum:** "Presidio Hill School was founded on progressive principles as an alternative to existing public schools and traditional private schools. Today, Presidio Hill continues to provide a progressive program that encourages independent thinking, questioning, experimenting and evaluating. The three R's are taught not as ends in themselves but as tools for the child to lead a creative life."

•**Admission Requirements and Procedure:** Interested parents meet the director and tour the school. Following tours, applicants may schedule an interview with teacher, child, and parents. Acceptance of applicants generally closes in February. Notifications are sent in mid-March of school year preceding September entrance.

•**Most Recent Fee Schedule:** Tuition ranges from $3,575 to $4,565 per year depending on age of student. Tuition aid is available.

RIVENDELL SCHOOL

4501 Irving Street (at 46th Avenue), San Francisco, CA 94122

(415) 566-7454

•**Co-directors:** Li Moon and Kaye Cofini

Rivendell was established in 1970 and currently has 60 children enrolled in a non-graded, individualized program for students from kindergarten through sixth grade. The teacher-student ratio is 1:10. School hours are 9:00 a.m. to 3:00 p.m. with extended day care available. Rivendell offers a summer session. Field trips are an integral part of the program.

Registered with the State Department of Education. Recognized by Pacific Region Association of Alternative Schools.

•**Philosophy/Goals/Curriculum:** "Our purpose is to provide an intellectually stimulating and emotionally supportive environment, to foster creativity in all its forms and to encourage each child to take responsibility for his/her own learning. We seek to provide the balance of structure and freedom that supports each child and enables him or her to enjoy the search for personal knowledge. We expect students to assume responsibility for their lives appropriate to their age and development. We listen to our children and respect their point of view. We offer individualized instruction in reading, writing and mathematics; a strong laboratory science program; computers, foreign language, music and art; weekly swimming and camping trips."

•**Admission Requirements and Procedure:** Admission is based on teacher observation rather than formal testing. Appropriate standardized tests are then used to develop each child's program and measure progress throughout the year.

•**Most Recent Fee Schedule:** Tuition: $3,150 per year. There are some partial scholarships available. Extended day care is $2.50 per hour.

SACRED HEART CATHEDRAL PREPARATORY

1055 Ellis Street, San Francisco, CA 94109

(415) 775-6626

•**Principal:** Brother Christopher Brady, F.S.C.

Owned by the Roman Catholic Archdiocese and directed by the Christian Brothers and Daughters of Charity, Sacred Heart Cathedral Preparatory is the first high school to offer Catholic coeducation to the youth of San Francisco. Building on the years of service to education by the two orders, Sacred Heart Cathedral Prep is the culmination of twenty years of active cooperation between Sacred Heart High School and Cathedral High School. It has 940 boys and girls enrolled in a college preparatory program in grades nine through twelve. The average class size is 29, with 55 credentialed teachers on the faculty. School hours are 8:00 a.m. to 2:05 p.m. A summer school is also part of the program. There is a dress code. Accredited by WASC.

•**Philosophy/Goals/Curriculum:** "Sacred Heart Cathedral Preparatory is a co-educational institution intent upon offering an exellent Catholic, college preparatory program, with a solid sequential curriculum of religious education, the liberal arts, and physical and life sciences. Sacred Heart Cathedral Prep offers honors programs at all grade levels and Advanced Placement courses at the eleventh and twelfth grades."

•**Admission Requirements and Procedure:** The annual admission process for prospective ninth grade boys and girls begins in October of each year with an annual Open House for all interested parents and students. Applications will be accepted until the time of the entrance examination in January and after that by special arrangement. The Admissions Committee will evaluate recommendations, transcripts, tests, and personal interviews during February. Parents and students will be notified of their acceptance by mid-March. Transfer students (for tenth, eleventh, and twelfth grades) may make application by contacting the Admissions Office at any time.

•**Most Recent Fee Schedule:** Tuition: $3,600 per year; extensive tuition awards are available based on applicant's scholarship and family need.

SACRED HEART GRAMMAR SCHOOL

735 Fell Street (at Fillmore), San Francisco, CA 94117
(415) 621-8035

•**Principal:** Sister Cathryn deBack, O.P.

Sacred Heart Grammar School was founded in 1926 and has an enrollment of 200 students, kindergarten to eighth grade with eight full-time teachers and one part-time teacher. Average class size is 25. Teachers are credentialed and average ten years of experience. School hours are from 8:00 a.m. to 3:00 p.m. with extended day care available until 6:00 p.m. Uniforms are required.

Accredited by WCEA.

•**Philosophy/Goals/Curriculum:** "Sacred Heart Grammar School is a Catholic parish school serving primarily the Western Addition neighborhood. It has a basic curriculum with some ungraded programs designed to meet the individual needs of students. A Christian environment emphasizing the basic sanctity and dignity of each student is provided."

•**Admission Requirements and Procedure:** Testing begins in April – by appointment.

•**Most Recent Fee Schedule:** Tuition is $90 per month. Extended care is $50 per month.

ST. ANTHONY'S SCHOOL

299 Precita Avenue (at Folsom), San Francisco, CA 94110
(415) 648-2008

•**Principal:** Sister JoAnn Kozloski, O.P.

St. Anthony's School has been in existence since 1894. There are 300 students enrolled from kindergarten through eighth grade. Average class size is 34, with nine teachers on the staff. School hours are from 8:15 a.m. to 2:45 p.m. Uniforms are required. Extended daycare is provided on a limited basis until 6:00 p.m. for St. Anthony students.

Accredited by WCEA.

•**Philosophy/Goals/Curriculum:** "We endeavor to educate the whole child (spiritually, intellectually and emotionally)."

•**Admission Requirements and Procedure:** Please call St. Anthony's School for information.

•**Most Recent Fee Schedule:** Please call St. Anthony's School for information.

ST. DOMINIC SCHOOL

2445 Pine Street (between Pierce and Steiner), San Francisco, CA 94115
(415) 346-9500

•**Principal:** Sister M. Annette Sheaffer

St. Dominic School has an enrollment of 195 students from kindergarten
through sixth grade. Seven credentialed teachers serve on the staff, with average
class size from 25 to 30 students. School hours are from 8:20 a.m. to 2:45 p.m.,
with extended care available until 5:45 p.m. Uniforms are required.

Accredited by WCEA.

•**Philosophy/Goals/Curriculum:** "Saint Dominic is a Catholic elementary school
serving students from a predominantly black, inner-city community. The school
staff endeavors to understand and satisfy the particular and unique needs of the
students by affirming their worth as individuals and as members of a rich, beauti-
ful, and significant culture. It works to help students come to value judgments
based on Christian principles. The staff is committed to supporting each individual student so that he or she becomes a self-disciplined, thinking and considerate
person." Students are educated in a traditional classroom setting through a basic
curriculum and are assisted in becoming secure in their skills and motivated
to expand their knowledge of the world. Religious goals, cultural and social
goals, academic goals, and psychological goals are formulated within the above
philosophy."

•**Admission Requirements and Procedure:** Application, interview, and non-
standardized, basic skills test scheduled by appointment.

•**Most Recent Fee Schedule:** One child: $900 per year; Two or more children:
$675 per year; Supply fee for each child: $90.

ST. EMYDIUS SCHOOL

301 De Montfort Avenue (one block off Ocean Avenue at Jules), San Francisco,
CA 94112
(415) 333-4877

•**Principal:** Leo Delucci

St. Emydius School has been in existence since 1939. Current enrollment is
220 students from kindergarten through eighth grade. Average class size is 26.

There are eight full-time and three part-time credentialed teachers, three with Master's degrees. School hours are from 8:05 a.m. to 2:45 p.m. Extended day care is available until 6:00 p.m. Uniforms are required.

Accredited by WASC and WCEA.

•**Philosophy/Goals/Curriculum:** "St. Emydius School exists to assist the students by offering a comprehensive education to meet the needs of the students. It encourages them to grow in an intellectual knowledge of their faith through religious instruction; to develop an increasing awareness of the religious dimensions of all of life's problems; and to seek an environment of Christian faith and charity. Subjects taught are religion, mathematics, reading, language, arts, social studies, science, spelling, art, music, penmanship, government, physical education." A full school computer program is offered, as well as a variety of extra curricular activities.

•**Admission Requirements and Procedure:** Application begins January 15 each year. No final deadline. Notification is immediately after testing and interview.

•**Most Recent Fee Schedule:** Tuition for one child is $1,450 for contributing church members; $1,750 for non-contributing. Tuition is prorated for additional children and payable on a ten-month schedule, quarterly, bi-annually, or annually. Day care for kindergarteners is $150 per month, for gradeschool children, $110 per month. Financial aid is available based on need.

ST. GABRIEL PARISH SCHOOL

2550 41st Avenue (between Ulloa and Vicente), San Francisco, CA 94116
(415) 566-0314

•**Principal:** Sister M. Pauline, S.M.

St. Gabriel Parish School has an enrollment of 453 students from kindergarten through eighth grade. Average class size is 25. All 22 teachers are credentialed. School hours are from 8:15 a.m. to 3:00 p.m. Uniforms are required. A summer school program is available.

Accredited and certified by WCEA.

•**Philosophy/Goals/Curriculum:** "St. Gabriel Parish School aims to promote the religious, intellectual, moral, cultural and physical development of each child to prepare him or her to live as an educated and fully integrated person in our complex American society and eventually to attain his or her eternal destiny. St.

Gabriel's prepares students for the future through value-oriented education by fulfilling the Archdiocesan academic requirements; laying a strong foundation of basic skills, especially reading, writing, math and religion and by fostering the Christian vision of persons and society. Extra programs offered include Extended Care, remedial services, individual and family counseling, computer instruction, primary motor skills (grades K through two), after school sports (grades four through eight), English as a Second Language, speech, drama and music."

•**Admission Requirements and Procedure:** Applications are available starting in January. Kindergarten testing begins in February by appointment. Testing for grades one through eight is after Easter. Parents are notified by the last week in April.

•**Most Recent Fee Schedule:** Tuition for one child: $1,545 plus thirty parent volunteer hours; or $1,741 (without parent volunteer hours.)

ST. IGNATIUS COLLEGE PREPARATORY SCHOOL
2001 37th Avenue (at Quintara), San Francisco, CA 94116
(415) 731-7500

•**Principal:** Mario Prietto, S.J.

St. Ignatius was founded by the Jesuit Fathers in 1855 as Saint Ignatius Academy, and brings a 134-year history of distinguished service to San Francisco. It has an enrollment of 1,240 students in grades nine through twelve. SI welcomed its first coed freshman class in the fall of 1989. Average class size is 26, with 80 credentialed teachers. School hours are from 8:30 a.m. to 2:15 p.m. A summer school program is provided. Bus service to Marin County and the Peninsula is available. There is a dress code.

Accredited by WASC.

•**Philsophy/Goals/Curriculum:** "St. Ignatius offers an extensive college preparatory curriculum. In addition, students are required to participate in theology classes, campus ministry program, student activities, and a community service requirement. Last year, ninety-nine percent of the student body went on to college."

•**Admission Requirements and Procedure:** "The admissions cycle begins in the fall. Eighth grade students are encouraged to visit our campus and attend morning classes. Two open houses are held each fall on the last Sunday of October and on the third Sunday of November. Applications are due the first week of January and applicants must sit for an entrance exam given by any of the 17 Catholic Schools in the San Francisco Archdiocese, January 6, 13, or 20. School records and recommendations must be received by mid-February and students are notified of their acceptance by March 10."

•**Most Recent Fee Schedule:** Tuition: $3,700 per year. Financial assistance is offered to any student with demonstrated need. Students should contact the Principal's Office for details.

ST. JOHN'S ELEMENTARY SCHOOL

925 Chenery Street (between Burnside and Chilton), San Francisco, CA 94131
(415) 584-8383

•**Principal:** Sister Susan Barry, O.S.U.

St. John's was founded in 1917 and serves 270 students, kindergarten through eighth grade. Average class size is 30 to 35. All of the teachers are credentialed. School hours are from 8:30 a.m. to 3:00 p.m., with extended care from 7:00 a.m. before school to 6:00 p.m. after school. Uniforms are required.

Accredited by WCEA.

•**Philosophy/Goals/Curriculum:** "The purpose of our school is to create an environment in which its students can develop Catholic Christian values as they receive quality education – morally, spiritually, socially, physically and academically. We endeavor to develop in the student a positive sense of self-worth along with respect for all individuals. The student will begin to discover what part he or she will play in the world through participation in and contribution to the life of the family, parish and civic communities. Trying to live a life of faith does bring about a sense of self-worth, communication and love for all concerned."

•**Admission Requirements and Procedure:** The family files an application form, accompanied by a $10 application fee. The family then is interviewed by the pastor and the principal. Students in grades one through eight are academically tested to determine strengths and weaknesses, and to be sure that St. John's is the best school for the student.

•**Most Recent Fee Schedule:** Full-day kindergarten: $1,600 per year; Grades one through eight: $1,300 - $1,600 per year. Scholarships and tuition aid are available for those who are Catholic and live in St. John's Parish.

ST. JOHN URSULINE SCHOOL

4056 Mission Street (near Bosworth), San Francisco, CA 94122

(415) 586-6333

•**Principal:** Sister Shirley Ann Garibaldi, OSU

St. John Ursuline has been housed in its present building since 1957 and has an enrollment of 166 girls in grades nine through twelve. Most of the 17 full-time and two part-time teachers are credentialed and have advanced degrees. Average class size is between 15 and 20. There are three basic programs: college preparatory, business education, and general education. A summer school program is available for enrolled or incoming students. School hours are 8:15 a.m. to 3:00 p.m. Uniforms are required.

Accredited by WASC.

•**Philosophy/Goals/Curriculum:** "The aim of St. John Ursuline is to educate the whole person in an atmosphere of openness and sensitivity. Students are treated as individuals. We believe that for this education to be effective students must accept responsibility for learning. We recognize the role that parents should play in education, and we constantly seek their collaboration, hence encouraging family unity."

•**Admission Requirements and Procedure:** For incoming freshmen, applications are accepted at any time, although none are processed until after the Placement Test has been given (January 6 and January 20). Acceptance notification date: March 8.

•**Most Recent Fee Schedule:** Tuition: $270 per month. Both need-based and merit-based financial aid grants are awarded each year.

ST. JOSEPH SCHOOL

220 10th Street (at Howard), San Francisco, CA 94103

(415) 431-1206

•**Director:** Rev. Fred Al. Bitanga

•**Principal:** Sister M. Cornelia C. Ramirez, R.V.M.

St. Joseph School, founded in 1867, serves 287 students from kindergarten through eighth grade. Average class size is 30, with credentialed teachers on the

staff. School hours are from 8:20 a.m. to 3:00 p.m. Extended day care is available.
Uniforms are required.

Accredited by WCEA and WASC.

•**Philosophy/Goals/Curriculum:** St. Joseph School is a Christian community
located in the South of Market district of San Francisco. It serves children from
different parishes throughout the entire Bay Area. The staff is committed to the
mission of providing quality Catholic education. "At St. Joseph School, we try
our best to create an atmosphere of love and unity to support this value-based
educational program. We strive to assist parents with their duty to help their
children become responsible, Gospel-oriented Christians. Instruction in religious
truth and values is an integral part of the school program. It is not one more
subject alongside the rest, but the underlying reality. We believe that each child is
valuable and must be given the opportunity to develop the talents God has given
him or her; that the process of education involves the development of the whole
person. The elementary curriculum guidelines from the Department of Education
in the Archdiocese of San Francisco are followed. The four basic areas of curriculum foundations (epistemology, society/culture, the individual and learning
theories) constitute the primary forces that influence and control the content and
organization of the curriculum."

•**Admission Requirements and Procedure:** Entrance tests; Immunization
records; Birth certificate/Baptismal record; and Report card.

•**Most Recent Fee Schedule:** Kindergarten through eight, one child: $1,100 per
year; Grades K through eight, two or more children: $1,750 per year. Tuition aid
is available.

ST. MONICA SCHOOL

5020 Geary Boulevard (at 24th Avenue), San Francisco, CA 94121
(415) 751-9564

•**Co-principals:** Sister Sally Thompson; Sister Stephanie Rose Stemberger

St. Monica School was founded in 1919 and has an enrollment of 336 students,
kindergarten through eighth grade. It is staffed by twelve Sisters of the Holy
Names and lay teachers, all credentialed. Average class size is 40. School hours
are from 8:15 a.m. to 2:50 p.m. Uniforms are required.

Accredited by WASC and WCEA.

•**Philosophy/Goals/Curriculum:** "We believe every facet of life is important: spiritual, physical, intellectual, emotional. We believe every child is unique and valuable, for his or her life comes from God. We believe one purpose of life is to improve the quality of life for all people everywhere. If we have helped a child become more human, more understanding of others, more trusting in life's ultimate value, more hopeful, then we have prepared that child for life. St. Monica School emphasizes Christian formation and values in all courses of study. These include religion, language arts, mathematics, science, social studies, music, art, physical education and family life."

•**Admission Requirements and Procedure:** Children must be fluent in English, able to function in a regular classroom, and supportive of school philosophy. Registration is the first two Sundays in March. Acceptance is in the middle of April.

•**Most Recent Fee Schedule:** Catholics in Parish: $1,000 per year for the first child and $1,200 per year for two or more children. Catholics outside of Parish: $1,100 per year for the first child and $1,300 per year for two or more children. Non-Catholics: $1,300 for the first child and $1,500 per year for two or more children. Scholarships in special circumstances.

ST. PAUL'S HIGH SCHOOL

317 29th Street (at Church), San Francisco, CA 94131
(415) 648-0505

•**Principal:** Sister Maureen O'Brien, BVM

St. Paul's was founded in 1917 and has an enrollment of 180 girls in grades nine through twelve. There are 13 full-time and three part time teachers, most of whom are credentialed and hold advanced degrees. The average class size ranges from nine to twelve students. The curriculum includes three programs: college preparatory, general education, and business education. School hours are 8:20 a.m. to 2:30 p.m. Uniforms are required.

Accredited by WASC and The Western Catholic Education Association.

•**Philosophy/Goals/Curriculum:** "St. Paul's High School is dedicated to the development of faith, the pursuit of knowledge, and the practice of love. As a Catholic center of learning, we are in partnership with the family and the Church as we contribute to the process of the formation of the whole person. The functions of our school are to be a Christian community where students may experience, by word and example, what it means to be a Catholic Christian; to offer an academic program that meets the needs of our students and to prepare them for their future life; and to provide a variety of opportunities for spiritual, intellectual, emotional, aesthetic, social, and physical development."

•**Admission Requirements and Procedure:** Admissions criteria include performance to best of ability in elementary school, a good attendance record, a positive disciplinary record, and seriousness about receiving a Catholic education. Priority application date: January 6 (acceptance notification date: March 10) then on through the summer. Admission materials include application form, registration fee, and STS High School Placement Test.

•**Most Recent Fee Schedule:** Tuition: $2,800. Monthly tuition payment schedule is available. The school has a substantial commitment to financial aid based on need, and three merit scholarships are awarded each year.

ST. PAULUS LUTHERAN SCHOOL

888 Turk Street (at Gough), San Francisco, CA 94102
(415) 673-8088

•**Principal:** John W. Lueck, M.A.

St. Paulus Lutheran School was founded in 1872. It serves pre-kindergarten through eighth grade. Enrollment is 171 students. Class size is limited to 25 in grades Kindergarten through six and 27 in grades seven through eight. All teachers have teaching credentials and some have master's degrees. Classes are self-contained through sixth grade, and academically departmentalized in seventh and eighth grades. Students are required to wear uniforms. School hours are from 8:30 a.m. to 3:00 p.m. Extended day care is available until 6 p.m. The summer school program includes individual tutoring, enrichment, and recreation.

St. Paulus Lutheran School is accredited and licensed by the Lutheran Church.

•**Philosophy/Goals/Curriculum:** The four R's are emphasized at St. Paulus Lutheran School: Reading, 'Riting, 'Rithmetic and Religion. Instruction in religion is not sectarian, but meant to support Christian faith and life. The school stresses "the importance of living together as human beings . . . to care for and to respect ourselves and one another . . . to act responsibly as human beings. Each child is very important to us. We use all the resources available to aid the student in growth. Parents are involved to a great extent in the education of their children. The teaching curriculum is the standard curriculum. The basics – reading and mathematics – are especially emphasized. Social studies, science, language and spelling are also stressed." Art, music, and athletics are offered. Religion classes and weekly morning chapel services are part of the program.

•**Admission Requirements and Procedure:** An application form is submitted, followed by an interview with the Principal. An evaluation is made of all the students on a selected date to determine how they will fit in with the class at their grade level.

•**Most Recent Fee Schedule:** Application fee: $50 (nonrefundable); Education fee: $200 (nonrefundable); Preschool annual tuition: $240 per month, full-day and $140 per month, half-day; Grades Kindergarten through eight annual tuition: $1,400 first child; $140 discount for siblings and church members.

ST. THOMAS THE APOSTLE SCHOOL

3801 Balboa Street (at 39th Avenue), San Francisco, CA 94121
(415) 221-2711

•**Principal:** Kathleen Hume Hanley

St. Thomas the Apostle School was established in 1948 and has an enrollment of 255 students, kindergarten through the eighth grade. Nine full-time and five part-time teachers are on staff and have credentials and/or Master's degrees. Average class size is 28. School hours are from 8:05 a.m. to 2:45 p.m. Extended day care is available until 6:00 p.m.

Accredited by WASC and WCEA.

•**Philosophy/Goals/Curriculum:** "The school provides a solid academic foundation in a Christian atmosphere. . . . Kindergarten through fifth grade are in self-contained classrooms; sixth through eighth grades are departmentalized. Formal religious instruction and a spirit of respect and service form Christian students. Parent and faculty cooperate in building a shared Catholic community in which children learn and grow. . . . Each child is valued as a unique person with individual gifts and needs. The staff encourages children to develop a strong self-esteem, and to make an active contribution to the school community. Our rigorous academic program provides an opportunity to discover the joy of learning and the pleasure of intellectual, cultural and physical activity."

•**Admission Requirements and Procedure:** Kindergarten applicants are screened for readiness. Children must be five years old before December 1 of kindergarten year. All incoming students are tested, parents are interviewed, and a tour of the school is given. Parents are notified of acceptance within a week of testing.

•**Most Recent Fee Schedule:** $140 - $160 per month for ten months, depending upon grade level, and due the fifteenth of each month, August - May. Archdiocesan family grant, parish scholarship for Catholic students, and one year financial aid up to $500 available, based on need.

SAN FRANCISCO CHINESE PARENTS' COMMITTEE SCHOOL

843 Stockton Street (at Clay), San Francisco, CA 94108
(415) 391-5564

•**Principal:** Emma Lee

The San Francisco Chinese Parents' Committee School was founded in 1971. It has 200 students enrolled, pre-kindergarten through sixth grade. Average class size is 25, with credentialed, experienced, and qualified teachers on the staff. School hours are from 8:30 a.m. to 3:00 p.m. A summer school program is provided. School uniforms are required.

Registered with the State Department of Education.

•**Philosophy/Goals/Curriculum:** "To see each child as an individual and to help him meet his individual educational needs; to guide children in reaching the educational goals of their grade level during the school year; to help children develop a sense of personal worth; to help children continue to develop the self-discipline and personal values begun in the home which will assist them in entering the larger world community; to keep parents well informed of their child's progress."

•**Admission Requirements and Procedure:** The school admits children throughout the school year. Children are admitted on the basis of an interview, previous school records, and an entrance examination to determine eligibility.

•**Most Recent Fee Schedule:** Pre-kindergarten: $80 per session (not included in the family plan); Kindergarten through sixth grade: $75 per month for one child, $135 per month for two children (family plan), $190 per month for three children, $220 per month maximum for families with four or more children. Registration, book, and insurance fees not included.

SAN FRANCISCO DAY SCHOOL

350 Masonic Avenue (at Golden Gate), San Francisco, CA 94118
(415) 931-2422

•**Head of School:** Nancy S. Boettiger

San Francisco Day School opened with grades kindergarten through second
grade in September 1981. It now serves kindergarten through eighth grade.
Current enrollment is 369 students. Typical class size is 22, with a teacher-student
ratio of 1:11. Teachers are credentialed or have higher degrees in specialized
teaching areas. School hours are 8:30 a.m. to 2:15 p.m. for kindergarten and first
grade, 8:30 a.m. to 3:15 p.m. for second and third grade, and 8:20 a.m. to 3:30 p.m.
for grades four through eight. An extended day program with a variety of activities is available from dismissal to 6:00 p.m. daily and all day during most vacation
periods. A four-week summer program in the arts is offered.

San Francisco Day School is a member of NAIS and CAIS.

•**Philosophy/Goals/Curriculum:** "The primary purpose of San Francisco Day
School is to educate and nurture its students according to the highest standards of
academic excellence and behavior. Each child is valued as a unique person with
individual gifts and needs. Our faculty welcomes the challenge of educating
children of varying abilities while expecting all students to strive to do their best.
The academic program provides the opportunity for each child to progress at his or
her own pace and to discover the joy of learning and the pleasure of lifelong
pursuits – intellectual, cultural, physical. The school seeks a partnership with each
child's family, based on mutual respect, trust and open communication."

•**Admission Requirements and Procedure:** Admission to San Francisco Day
School is based on personal and academic qualifications. The regular admissions
procedure includes a conference with parents, a visit with and obervation of the
child in a social setting, an evaluation of previous school records, and entrance
tests. Kindergarten applications close on January 20; kindergarten parents are
notified on March 15.

•**Most Recent Fee Schedule:** $4,950 - $6,150 per year depending upon grade
level. Financial assistance is available on the basis of family need.

SAN FRANCISCO HEARING AND SPEECH CENTER

1234 Divisadero Street (between Ellis and Eddy), San Francisco, CA 94115
(415) 921-7658

- **Executive Director:** Rayford C. Reddell, Ph.D.
- **Aphasic Program Director:** Mary Ann Ceriotti
- **Director, Hearing Impaired Program:** Gloria Sevilla, M.A.

The San Francisco Hearing and Speech Center was founded in 1963. Fourteen students, aged three to ten, are enrolled in two aphasic classes. The teachers are credentialed. School hours are 9:00 a.m. to 3:00 p.m. The center also has an audiology program, speech pathology program, research program, individual therapy, and preschool class for hearing impaired children.

Accredited by the American Speech, Language and Hearing Association Board of Examiners and registered with the State Department of Education.

- **Philosophy/Goals/Curriculum:** Full-time, ungraded classes are offered for children with aphasia and related language disorders. Class size is limited to eight students, with intensive instruction in speech, writing, language structure, and understanding spoken and written language. "Hearing impaired children are seen beginning with the detection of a hearing loss. A combination of center-based and home-based services meet the special needs of children under three years of age and their families. Curriculum includes the development of auditory skills, speechreading skills, speech, receptive language, expressive language, sign language (where appropriate), and parent education. Three to five year olds attend preschool classes five days per week. Individual therapy can be arranged for older children. All instruction provided by credentialed teachers and therapists. Following initial evaluation and consultation, families select either Oral/Aural or Total Communication program for their child."
- **Admission Requirements and Procedure:** The Center, a non-profit community service agency, accepts children and adults with hearing, speech, or language disorders. Enrollment in self-contained classes or in individual therapy is based upon a child's age and needs. Families are accepted immediately upon discernment of the appropriateness of the program.
- **Most Recent Fee Schedule:** Tuition for aphasic class is $12,500 per year; PL 94-142 funding is accepted. Fees for the programs for the hearing impaired are set on

a sliding scale according to family income and expenses. No one is refused services of the Center because of inability to pay.

SAN FRANCISCO JUNIOR ACADEMY

66 Geneva Avenue (between Phelan and Howth), San Francisco, CA 94112
(415) 585-5550

•**Principal:** Leon Stickney

San Francisco Junior Academy was established in 1929, and has an enrollment of 116 students in grades kindergarten through ten. The average class size is 20. The nine teachers on the staff are credentialed. School hours are 8:30 a.m. to 2:30 p.m. for the first and second grade, and 8:30 a.m. to 3:15 p.m. for the remainder of the school. Prayer and Bible Study are an integral part of the total school program. Uniforms are required. The school is proud of its strong music program.

Accredited by Pacific Union Conference of Seventh-Day Adventists Educational Department.

•**Philosophy/Goals/Curriculum:** "San Francisco Junior Academy was founded by the Seventh-Day Adventist Church. It is the purpose of the SFJA to provide for its students a Christ-centered program of studies and activities that will harmoniously balance the development of the physical, mental and spiritual needs of the student. We believe that there is security in defined limits. Children want discipline and respond to it if it is administered with love. Our goal is accomplished by offering sound instruction in the basic required subjects; by encouraging an appreciation for good music, fine arts, various sciences and physical fitness."

•**Admission Requirements and Procedure:** Acceptance in first grade will be dependent upon readiness testing and demonstrated ability to handle first-grade material. Students transferring to San Francisco Junior Academy will be placed in the grade where they can keep up with the work in a satisfactory manner.

•**Most Recent Fee Schedule:** Fees range from $1,080-$1,380 per year (depending upon grade level) for constituent members to $1,400-$1,850 per year per child (depending upon grade level) for non-constituent families.

THE SAN FRANCISCO SCHOOL

300 Gaven Street (at Boylston), San Francisco, CA 94134

(415) 239-5065

- **Director:** Terry Edely

    The San Francisco School was founded in 1966. The school has three levels: the Montessori preschool, ages three to five, the elementary school, grades one to five, and the middle school, grades six to eight. The teacher-student ratio is 1:12. School hours are 9:00 a.m. to 3:00 p.m. The extended care program hours are 7:30 a.m. to 6:00 p.m. Current enrollment is 207. A day camp program is provided in the summer.

- **Philosophy/Goals/Curriculum:** "The philosophy of the San Francisco School is rooted in a commitment to each child's growing sense of responsibility, which is fostered from the child's earliest experience in the Montessori-based preschool. Later, as children progress to the elementary program, teachers stress academic skills while designing activities that require children to be resourceful, cooperative and responsible for the quality of their work. Structured and challenging academic instruction is balanced with open-ended projects which encourage children to use their full complement of skills and experience. The curriculum includes a rich creative arts program of art, music, dance and drama; cultural studies; and an experiential science program. Foreign language instruction begins at second grade. The middle school program includes computer studies and community experience activities. Throughout the child's school experience, process and content are balanced so that students remain capable and enthusiastic learners."

- **Admission Requirements and Procedure:** Please call to request a brochure and an observation appointment. Applications are distributed at this observation. Students are accepted on the basis of a family interview with classroom teachers, and a student visit to the classroom. Admissions testing is informal. Applications are accepted all year. Applications due date is February 1. Notification of acceptance is in March.

- **Most Recent Fee Schedule:** Preschool: $4,000 per year; Elementary school: $4,250 - $4,350 per year; Extended day care: $2.85 per hour. Tuition includes lunch, books, and field trips. Monthly payments and Tuition Aid are available.

SAN FRANCISCO UNIVERSITY HIGH SCHOOL

3065 Jackson Street (between Baker and Lyon), San Francisco, CA 94115
(415) 346-8400

•**Headmaster:** Peter T. Esty

San Francisco University High School, founded in 1973, opened to students as
a college preparatory, coeducational day school for grades nine through twelve.
There are currently 385 students enrolled with 51 full-time and nine part-time
teachers. Class size averages 14 students. School hours are 8:10 a.m. to 3:10 p.m.
Students have opportunities to pursue on or off campus independent study for a
term or longer. Serious language students may qualify for various travel-study
programs. The school offers a summer academic enrichment program for public
school seventh and eighth graders. A neat and clean appearance is required.

Accredited by WASC.

•**Philosophy/Goals/Curriculum:** "Created to serve young men and women of
above-average intellectual ability, S.F. University High School strives to nourish
and encourage a love of learning so that graduates may enjoy full, meaningful
lives, and so that the community may benefit from the development of creative,
capable leaders. The School is committed to the students' welfare and total
emotional, moral, physical and intellectual growth."

•**Admission Requirements and Procedure:** Admission procedures include
completion of an application packet (student essay, recommendations, and
transcripts), an interview and visit, and results of the SSAT. Application should
be completed by January 26 for mid-March acceptance.

•**Most Recent Fee Schedule:** Tuition: $8,450; Activities fee: $60; Books and
supplies: $250 - $300 per year. Financial aid is available based on need, not merit.
Application deadline for Parent's Financial Statement is January 26, and for tax
forms, February 16.

THE SAN FRANCISCO WALDORF SCHOOL

2938 Washington Street (between Broderick and Divisadero), San Francisco, CA
94115 (415) 931-2750

•**Administrative Chairperson:** Corinne Fendell

San Francisco Waldorf School opened its doors in September 1979. It is part of the Waldorf movement, consisting of over 300 schools throughout the world, founded by Dr. Rudolf Steiner in Europe in 1919. The school presently has 186 children in two kindergartens and grades one through eight. A class teacher ideally stays with one group of children from the first grade through the eighth grade. All teachers have a rigorous two-year training from a recognized Waldorf teacher training institute. School hours vary according to grade level. Extended day care is provided until 5:30 p.m. A summer school program is available.

Registered with the State Department of Education.

•**Philosophy/Goals/Curriculum:** "Waldorf education aims to integrate intellectual achievement with harmonious physical, mental and spiritual growth. We believe that an education that develops the full human and creative potential of the growing child is one of the most important gifts that parents can give to their children. Waldorf education stresses the need for harmony between school and home. Thus parents meet regularly with the teacher to discuss their children's development, class and home environment and other important issues.

"In Kindergarten great care is taken to provide an environment which engages the child's awakening senses through creative play and imaginative activities. In the grades, a wide spectrum of academic subjects is added, including the sciences and the humanities such as mathematics, English, botany, zoology, history, physics, physiology, chemistry, geography and foreign language. Artistic and practical activities occupy an important place in the curriculum."

•**Admission Requirements and Procedure:** Admission is by application on a space available basis. Parent cooperation in the Waldorf method is essential. Prospective students and parents are interviewed by teachers.

•**Most Recent Fee Schedule:** Tuition ranges from $3,900 to $4,500 per year depending upon grade level. Application fee and deposit required. Tuition assistance is available.

SANDPATHS ACADEMY

525 Bryant Street (between 3rd and 4th streets), San Francisco, CA 94107
(415) 495-7937

•**Directors:** Jim and Candace Cusack

Sandpaths Academy was founded in 1968 to meet the needs of emotionally disturbed and learning disabled students. There is a current enrollment of 26 students from eight to twenty-one years old. The teacher-student ratio is 1:4. All teachers hold special education credentials. School hours are from 8:30 a.m. to 2:30 p.m. Mondays through Thursdays, and from 8:30 a.m. to 1:30 p.m. on Fridays. Many of the students are involved in day treatment programs or work experience programs. There is a dress code. Summer school is mandatory.

Registered with the State Department of Education.

•**Philosophy/Goals/Curriculum:** "Sandpaths emphasizes a problem-solving approach, development of basic communication skills and social skills. A diagnostic-prescriptive approach is utilized to individualize the educational process for each student. An adaptive Montessori program, speech, art and movement therapy, and computer training augment the curriculum. The Middle School program is more flexible and individualized to meet specific needs. The High School program is designed to enable students to meet state mandated graduation requirements. The overall goal of the school is for the students to become self-sufficient and independently functioning and to recognize their own worth and dignity. Individual and group counseling as well as family support services facilitate the educational process.

•**Admission Requirements and Procedure:** Most students are referred by the school district or other outside agencies. There is an interview and education assessment.

•**Most Recent Fee Schedule:** Funding is provided by Bay Area school districts.

STAR OF THE SEA SCHOOL

360-9th Avenue (at Geary Blvd.), San Francisco, CA 94118
(415) 221-8558

•**Principal:** Sister Rosemarie Carroll

Star of the Sea opened in 1909. Three hundred kindergarten to eighth grade students are enrolled. Nine full-time and three part-time credentialed teachers are on staff, with an average class size of 34. School hours are from 8:10 a.m. to 2:45 p.m. Extended day care is available at the adjoining YMCA. Uniforms are required.

Accredited by WCEA and WASC.

•**Philosophy/Goals/Curriculum:** "Through its years of education, Star of the Sea is known for its strong academic curriculum. National test scores indicate the solid foundation that the students are given. The primary and intermediate grades are self-contained, while grades seven to eight are departmentalized. Courses include religion, math, English, reading, science, spelling, social studies, and physical education. Art, music, and computer classes are also offered through the year. The spirit of community is fostered by the Parent Volunteer Program and the Parent Guild."

• **Admission Requirements and Procedure:** Please contact the school for information.

• **Most Recent Fee Schedule:** "School tuition is announced prior to registration each year with due regard for the ability of families of all sizes to pay."

STERNE SCHOOL

2690 Jackson Street (at Scott), San Francisco, CA 94115
(415) 922-6081

• **Director:** Valerie Anthony

Sterne School was established as a special education school for children with learning disabilities in 1976. It has an enrollment of 36 middle school students and 24 high school students, sixth through twelfth grade. Maximum class size is 12. School hours are 9:00 a.m. to 2:30 p.m. for middle school and 8:00 a.m. to 2:30 p.m. for high school. There is a six-week summer session and a dress code.

Certified by the California State Department of Education.

• **Philosophy/Goals/Curriculum:** "Sterne School is a full day school for children with specific learning disabilities. The goal of the school is to assist children to achieve their fullest academic potential and to help them return to regular education programs.

The children receive instruction in reading, language arts, history, science, geography, physical education and some elective courses. Computer activities are used to reinforce and enrich the curriculum. The school provides a multi-sensory approach to teaching reading and spelling with heavy emphasis on language development and phonics. Instruction in math emphasizes understanding of underlying concepts and development of basic math skills.

Sterne School does not accept children with emotional or behavior problems. The school has a clearly defined code of behavior and the students are closely supervised at all times. The school emphasizes self-reliance, organization, and social responsibility."

•**Admission Requirements and Procedure:** The admission procedure begins in January for the following school year. The process starts with a phone call from the parent. Among the factors considered in reviewing a child for admission are the nature and extent of the learning disability, current level of academic achievement, ability to adapt to the routines and requirements of the school, and a family that can understand and support the goals of the school. Admission procedures require parents to attend a parent orientation and the child to be interviewed.

•**Most Recent Fee Schedule:** Middle school students: $5,050/year, if paid in two installments; $5,350 if paid in monthly installments. High school program: $5,450/year if paid in two installments; $5,750/year if paid in monthly installments.

STUART HALL FOR BOYS

2252 Broadway (between Fillmore and Webster), San Francisco, CA 94115
(415) 563-2900

•**Headmaster:** William H. Miller

One of the three Schools of the Sacred Heart, Stuart Hall for Boys was founded in 1956. It has 290 students from pre-kindergarten through eighth grade with thirty credentialed teachers. School hours are from 8:25 a.m. to 3:00 p.m., with extended day care available until 6:00 p.m. A summer school program is provided. Uniforms are required.

Accredited by WASC and CAIS.

•**Philosophy/Goals/Curriculum:** "Stuart Hall is bound with the other Sacred Heart schools across the country by their commitment to: Educate students to a faith which is relevant in a secularized world; develop a deep respect for intellectual values; instill a social awareness which impels to action; build community as a Christian value; foster personal growth in an atmosphere of wise freedom. Stuart Hall offers a strong academic program which challenges each student to work to his greatest potential and prepares him for entrance into the finest secondary schools. . . . Equally important to the academic program is the development of a child who has a strong sense of his own spirituality and relationship with God, who is physically fit, who feels good about himself, and who treats others with respect, patience, and understanding. . . . The Curriculum at Stuart Hall encompasses solid academic subjects—reading, writing, spelling, grammar, mathematics, social studies, science, and religion—as well as subjects that enrich the traditional course work—physical education, foreign language, music, art, computer, and outdoor education. The services of a school counselor and an educational thera-pist are also available to the students. A full array of school activities, community services, electives, and an interscholastic sports program of soccer, basketball, and baseball are also components of the program. . . ."

•**Admission Requirements and Procedure:** Acceptance into Stuart Hall is based on report cards, school recommendations, an entrance examination, and a personal interview with the Headmaster or a designated representative.

•**Most Recent Fee Schedule:** The tuition schedule ranges from $5,450 to $5,925 depending upon grade level. Tuition rates include fees. Financial aid is available for eligible students.

SYNERGY SCHOOL

975 Grove Street (near Steiner), San Francisco, CA 94117
(415) 567-6177

•**Admissions Director:** Elena Dillon

Synergy School, founded in 1973, is a non-profit independent school serving approximately 80 children in kindergarten through sixth grade. Average class size is 12 in the lower grades and 16 in grades three to six. All six teachers are creden-tialed. School hours are from 8:45 a.m. to 3:00 p.m. Day care is available from 3:00 p.m. to 6:00 p.m. An outdoor oriented summer program operates during the summer session.

Registered with the State Department of Education.

•**Philosophy/Goals/Curriculum:** "Synergy School provides a challenging and innovative curriculum that stresses academic excellence within a humanistic context. The emphasis is on skill-building, independent thinking, creative expression, cooperation, and development of self-esteem. With the small class size, children are given individual attention and ample opportunity to move ahead at their own pace. Field trips, including overnight camping, provide high-interest direct experiences. Teachers maintain close contact with parents through meetings, conferences, and a monthly newsletter. The parents contribute invalu-able energy to the multi-cultural program."

•**Admission Requirements and Procedure:** Synergy School is coeducational and open to children ages four and one-half to twelve. Four criteria are used in evaluating prospective students: the school's contribution towards the education and growth of the student, the student's contribution to the school, the family's compatibility with Synergy's Educational Philosophy, and the willingness of the parents to be involved in the school. Parents are encouraged to come in and see the school in session. If you are interested, please telephone for an appointment.
•**Most Recent Fee Schedule:** Tuition: $3,450 per year. Scholarships are available.

TOWN SCHOOL
2750 Jackson Street (at Scott), San Francisco, CA 94115
(415) 921-3747

•**Headmaster:** W. Brewster Ely, IV
The Town School for Boys was founded in 1938. It is an independent day school enrolling students from kindergarten through eighth grade. It has a capacity of 396 students. There are two heterogeneous classes at each grade level. Class size does not exceed 22 pupils. The daily schedule is from 8:30 a.m. to 12:30 p.m. or 3:00 pm. depending upon grade level. Friday is a minimum day. Day care is available. Town School runs a coeducational summer school open to non-Town School students.
Accredited by CAIS and WASC.
•**Philosophy/Goals/Curriculum:** "The purpose of the school is to provide education of superior quality to the end that habits of study and an appreciation of learning will endure throughout secondary school, college, and life thereafter. Although preparation for the more selective public and independent schools is by no means the sole objective, it nonetheless remains an ancillary one, and each year many graduates enroll in leading secondary schools throughout the country. The development of self-confidence through individual encouragement is funda-mental to the school philosophy and unreasonable academic pressure is not in harmony with this belief. Town does assert the importance of hard work and individual challenge, however; to do otherwise would be unfair to both boys and parents and would imply a view of life which would be both fatuous and unrealistic."

•**Admission Requirements and Procedure:** Kindergarten admission is based upon preschool reports, an interview, and readiness testing. Grade school applicants are required to be present on "Testing Day" (part of selected independent school consortium).

•**Most Recent Fee Schedule:** A non-refundable registration fee is charged all applicants. If a student is accepted, it will be credited to the second semester tuition. Tuition is from $4,300 to $6,500 per year depending upon grade level. A $100 activity fee is charged for equipment for special projects and field trips.

THE URBAN SCHOOL OF SAN FRANCISCO

1563 Page Street, San Francisco, CA 94117

(415) 626-2919

•**Director:** Mark Salkind

The Urban School is an innovative, independent day school founded in 1966 and offering a demanding college preparatory program. With 175 boys and girls in grades nine through twelve and a faculty of 23, the student/teacher ratio is 10:1, and class size averages 15 students. Recently-expanded facilities (accessible to the disabled) house seminar-size classrooms, modern science laboratories, a theater, and art studios. Urban fields interscholastic teams in many sports and provides numerous extracurricular opportunities for student leaders, writers, and performers. Through extensive field work, community service, and internships, students explore and contribute to the larger community.

Accredited by WASC and CAIS.

•**Philosophy/Goals/Curriculum:** "Urban seeks to ignite a passion for learning and inspire its students to become self-motivated, enthusiastic participants in their education. The school strives to reflect the ethnic, racial, and socioeconomic diversity of the surrounding Bay Area communities. The block schedule of extended class periods promotes in-depth study and thoughtful discussion, and facilitates the use of valuable off-campus resources."

•**Admission Requirements and Procedure:** Urban seeks students with an enthusiastic approach to learning and a clear capacity for success in a challenging academic program. Admission procedures include completion of a student application, essay, recommendations, transcripts, SSAT results, student visit, and interview. Priority filing date is January 20; notifications are made March 10.

•**Most Recent Fee Schedule:** Application Fee: $30; Tuition: $8,050 per year; Books and materials: $400. Scholarships, based on need, are available.

WEST PORTAL LUTHERAN SCHOOL
200 Sloat Boulevard (between 19th Avenue and Portola), San Francisco, CA 94132 (415) 665-6330

•**Principal:** Shirley Merrill, M.A.

West Portal Lutheran School opened in September 1951. In 1974, an additional campus was added at 37th Avenue and Moraga Street, which provides facilities for grades one to three. Kindergarten and grades four through eight are located on the Sloat Boulevard Campus. Current enrollment is 560 students. The faculty numbers 25, with 30 students the typical class size. All teachers have degrees and credentials. School hours are from 8:30 a.m. to 2:45 p.m. for kindergarten through third grades; and 8:30 a.m. to 3:10 p.m. for grades four to eight. Day care is available until 6:00 p.m. A summer school program is provided. A dress code is enforced.

West Portal Lutheran School is an accredited Lutheran School and is registered with the State Department of Education.

•**Philosophy/Goals/Curriculum:** "The kindergarten and elementary grades are self-contained units, while seventh and eighth grades operate on a departmental basis. Every student takes part in weekly chapel services, daily devotion and other religious projects. The school maintains a high level of academic achievement. A strong emphasis is placed on academic subjects. The curriculum is enriched through field trips. The school has a computer lab, three libraries, audio-visual and video equipment, a gymnasium, and the use of two stages. Enrichment opportunities include Spanish, piano, and art classes. A strong sports program contributes to the development of well-rounded children."

•**Admission Requirements and Procedure:** First consideration is given to children of West Portal Lutheran Church members of over a year. Other children are placed according to Standardized Entrance Test results. Satisfactory academic and conduct grades from the present school are required. Parent and child must be receptive "to the fact that the Christian religion is taught in the classroom."

•**Most Recent Fee Schedule:** Entrance/Application Fee: $115. Tuition for kindergarten: $1,650 per ten-month term; Tuition for grades one through eight: $1,500 per ten-month term. Book fee: $100.

WILDSHAW INTERNATIONAL SCHOOL

385 Ashton Avenue (at Ocean), San Francisco, CA 94112
(415) 239-1115

•**Headmaster:** John S. Edwards

Wildshaw International School was founded in 1976. It has an enrollment of
75 students in grades six through twelve. The average class size is 12. The coeducational program is college preparatory, with an emphasis on study habits.
Field trips, both educational and recreational, are a regular feature. These include
a ski trip, and trips to Great America and Yosemite National Park. A small
summer school provides students with the opportunity to make up or earn extra
credit. There are no uniforms and there is no dress code.

The school is accredited by WASC and approved for foreign students, providing them with an I-20 form.

•**Philosophy/Goals/Curriculum:** "W.I.S. provides students with a varied college
prep program. It individualizes sufficiently to cater to the different needs of
students, including the gifted. It emphasizes foreign language and sound study
habits. Parents are actively encouraged to remain in close touch with the educational process. Almost 100 percent of its graduates go on to four-year colleges.
Wildshaw's success springs from its ability to stimulate student achievement, both
by respecting each student's individuality and by providing all students with a
consistent and meaningful program."

•**Admission Requirements and Procedure:** Students may apply year round,
provided there is space. Procedure includes two letters of reference, full set of
transcripts, CTBS/CAT scores, interview, and an optional day of visit. A parent
committee is available to offer further information to prospective and new parents.

•**Most Recent Fee Schedule:** Tuition: $4,920 payable in twelve installments of
$410. Tuition includes $168 toward books, insurance, yearbook, etc. Some
financial aid is available for students based on need and merit.

ZION LUTHERAN SCHOOL

495 9th Avenue (Geary Boulevard and Anza Street), San Francisco, CA 94118
(415) 221-7500

•**Principal:** Helen Hilst

Zion Lutheran School was established in 1947 to provide children of the congregation and the children of others with an education under Christian direction in a Christian environment. Currently 210 children are enrolled in kindergarten through eighth grade. Ten full-time and three part-time teachers are on the staff, with an average class size of 25. School hours are from 8:30 a.m. to 3:00 p.m. for grades one to eight. Extended day care is available from 3:00 p.m. to 6:00 p.m.. There is a weekly chapel program.

Registered with the State Department of Education.

•**Philosophy/Goals/Curriculum:** "The School endeavors to aid parents in following the Biblical command to bring up children 'in the nurture and admonition of the Lord.' Throughout the years we have perpetuated our primary purpose of giving our children a Christ-centered education and have maintained the scholastic standing of the school by continually revising our curriculum to meet the needs of today's children."

•**Admission Requirements and Procedure:** Call the school office to set up an appointment with the principal. Applications for the next school year are received from October 15 through January 30. Kindergarten acceptance letters are out by March 1; Grade one through eight are out by April 1.

•**Most Recent Fee Schedule:** Tuition: Kindergarten (full-day) through eighth grade is $1,475 per year. Registration for kindergarten: $350; Grades one through five: $375; grades seven to eight: $400. Outdoor Education for grades six through eight: $100. Computer classes for grades kindergarten through three: $75; grades four through eight: $100 per year. Extended day care is $900. Reduction in fees is available for three or more children in the same family. A sliding scale of fees is available in some cases.

Private Schools
MARIN COUNTY

ALLAIRE SCHOOL

50 El Camino Dr., Gamma 3, Corte Madera, CA 94925

(415) 927-2640

•**Director:** Mary Allaire

Allaire School was founded in January 1984 to serve students in grades one through eight who have learning problems that make it difficult for them to achieve their potential in a traditional classroom setting. The school is also for children whose readiness skills are delayed, in which case the pace of curriculum in a traditional setting might be too demanding. The average class size will be 12 students with a 1:3 teacher to pupil ratio. A summer school program is provided.

•**Philosophy/Goals/Curriculum:** "We each have a particular style of learning. This style is determined by our perceptual, cognitive, and motor abilities. Our strengths in these areas can be used to help compensate for our weaknesses, thereby permitting us to learn more efficiently. Academic subjects are taught based upon an educational evaluation of each student's skill levels, learning style and motivational needs. Reading, spelling and written language are highly integrated . . . math skills and concepts are applied in hands-on projects. Computer literacy is taught . . . social studies, science, music and art are included in the curriculum. Physical education involves students at their level of motor coordination and ability to follow rules."

•**Admission Requirements and Procedure:** Parents make an initial appointment to discuss enrollment. An application is filed which includes a school history, pertinent psychological data, and health records. An educational evaluation is made of the student's immediate learning needs. The current classroom composition regarding age range and social-emotional needs is an important factor in considering a student for the program.

•**Most Recent Fee Schedule:** Application fee: $100 (includes Educational Evaluation). Tuition: $6,250, one prepayment; $6,750, two installments; $7,000, monthly payments. *Tutorial:* $30-37 per 1 hour session. *Speech and Language Therapy:* Individual therapist's fees. *Summer Program:* $300-$400 per 2 week session depending on choice of classroom experience or 1:1 Tutorial. *Educational Evaluation:* $500. *Scholarships:* Families are assisted in applying for scholarships through local agencies.

BRANDEIS-HILLEL DAY SCHOOL

160 N. San Pedro Rd., San Rafael, CA 94903

(415) 472-1833

•**Director:** Frederick S. Nathan

•**Principal:** Susan Levinson

Brandeis-Hillel Day School of Marin was established in 1978 to provide quality education in General Studies and Hebrew/Judaic Studies. With an enrollment of 105 students and a capacity of 112 students, it serves students in kindergarten through sixth grade. School hours are 8:30 a.m. - 1:30 p.m. for kindergarten students and 8:30 a.m. - 3:15 p.m. for all other grades. There is an art, computer and library specialist one morning per week and physical education and music specialist twice per week. The school has 18 teachers, and limited transportation is provided. Brandeis-Hillel maintains another campus in San Francisco.

Accredited by WASC and membership in CAIS.

•**Philosophy/Goals/Curriculum:** "The philosophy of the school emerges from the values of Torah and Jewish tradition. The school creates a broad Jewish experience incorporating values and practices . . . from Jewish tradition and made relevant to contemporary life . . . ."

The curriculum consists of general studies (four hours daily), including language arts, reading, science, mathematics, social studies, physical education, dance, music, computers, and art; and Hebrew/Judaic studies (two hours daily) concentrating on the Hebrew language, the richness of Jewish history and literature, and the study of prayer, Torah, and Talmud.

"Shabbat and the holidays are observed and celebrated, thus making living Judaism an integral part of the child's school experience. The focus is on meeting the individual needs of each child. Knowledge, identification and experience are the objectives of the program."

•**Admission Requirements and Procedure:** An interview with the parents and the child, classroom observation, references, and academic testing to insure placement at the appropriate grade level.

•**Most Recent Fee Schedule:** Tuition: $3,000 per year; Enrichment: $250 per year; Building assessment: $200 per year; Parent Club: $50. Scholarships and loans are available.

THE BRANSON SCHOOL

Fernhill and Norwood Avenues, Ross, CA 94957

(415) 454-3612

Mailing Address: Box 887, Ross, CA 94957

•**Headmaster:** Richard P. Fitzgerald

•**Admissions Director:** Lee Carlson

The Branson School, founded in 1920, is a coeducational college preparatory day school for students in grades nine through twelve. Maximum enrollment is 320 students. Average class size is 15 students, and school hours are 8:15 a.m. to 3:00 p.m. A summer school program is available. There are sixteen campus buildings; seven house the 26 classrooms, the science and language laboratories, music, art and drama studies, the theatre and the 12,000-volume library. Bus transportation is provided from San Francisco.

Accredited by WASC.

•**Philosophy/Goals/Curriculum:** "The School offers a stimulating and vigorous college-preparatory curriculum, stressing the mastery of academic skills and concepts and their application, presented in an environment in which self-discipline and intellectual integrity are held in high esteem. The minimum requirement for graduation is a total of 16 units of academic credit (at least four per year). Each senior is required to complete an approved work-research creative or service project during the last three weeks of the academic year. Full year advanced placement study is available in all disciplines, and other college-level courses are readily accessible at nearby institutions. There are numerous athletic and extracurricular opportunities."

•**Admission Requirements and Procedure:** Initial inquiries can be made while the prospective Branson student is in the seventh grade. Application procedures, including submission of recommendations and an on-campus interview, begin in the Fall of the eighth-grade year and should be completed by mid-January. The nonrefundable application fee is $50. Notifications of acceptance are mailed early in March and parents reserve space within approximately three weeks.

•**Most Recent Fee Schedule:** Tuition: $8,250 per year. Full and partial scholarships are available.

CASCADE CANYON SCHOOL

2626 Sir Francis Drake Boulevard., Fairfax, CA 94930

(415) 459-3464

•**Director:** Anne-Marie Barar

Cascade Canyon School was founded in January 1980 and serves children from four to fourteen years of age in kindergarten through eighth grades. The school provides a broad general education as preparation for both public and private high schools. School hours are 8:30 am to 3:00 pm. There is an international overseas travel program available in the summer. This is a parent-run elementary school with current enrollment of 20 students. There are two full-time credentialed teachers and four part-time. Average class size is eight students. There is no dress code.

•**Philosophy/Goals/Curriculum:** "At the heart of our philosophy is the individual child. Each child learns and grows in a different way and has unique strengths. It is our role as a school to nurture that precious growth and challenge each child academically, physically and creatively to his or her best endeavors. The school provides an environment which stimulates learning in every area and permits each individual to learn at his or her own speed, tailoring our teaching to the preferred learning style of each student. We are able to provide an academic program suited to the needs of children of varying abilities and to ensure maximum individual attention, due to small class size. Cascade Canyon School welcomes parents as active participants in the classroom or on the Board and seeks a partnership with each family, based on open communication, mutual respect and trust. Our children have won artistic, academic and athletic awards and participate actively in the community.

"The academic program places emphasis on acquiring and developing the basic skills: reading, writing, computation, problem solving, and critical thinking. We emphasize equally fluency in at least one foreign language, a growing understanding of the world, its problems and peoples, and our place in it, and the development of artistic and creative talents.

"Throughout the school year, twice monthly field trips supplement and enrich classroom learning and opportunities abound for enrichment travel with several overnight expeditions and camping trips. In upper grades, our students also have the opportunity for overseas travel and community service projects in the Soviet

Union, Fiji, Australia and Europe."

The curriculum includes a literature-based reading program, language arts and creative writing, experiential learning mathematics program, global studies and world history, current events, foreign languages (French, Spanish, Russian and ESL), specialist taught music, arts and crafts courses, sciences, theater, physical education, computer learning, and extensive field trips.

•**Admission Requirements and Procedure:** Admission is available year round, based on an evaluation of previous school history, an interview with the family, and the child's participation in a typical school day. There is no entrance test. The school has an open door policy, encouraging families to visit the school and experience for themselves the type of opportunity provided.

•**Most Recent Fee Schedule:** Tuition ranges from $3,500 to $4,500 depending on the program, due in ten monthly payments beginning in May. Some work exchanges are available, but there are no scholarships

CHILD CENTER

P.O. Box 144, Kentfield, CA 94904
(415) 456-0440

•**Director:** Win Setrakian

The Child Center was formed in 1967 by a group of physicians, psychologists, and educators to serve the special needs of children with learning problems. The CHILD Center offers a full-time school for learning-handicapped students ages six through eighteen who have been unable to succeed in their previous school settings. Current enrollment is 18 students. Teacher-pupil ratio is 1:5.

Certified by the California State Department of Education to serve children funded under PL 94-142.

•**Philosophy/Goals/Curriculum:** "The CHILD Center School serves children with learning and/or behavior problems who need a solid framework for transition from failure in school to successful reentry into a public school program. It emphasizes highly structured individualized remediation for reading, language arts, and mathematics, coupled with a counseling program stressing improved peer and adult relationships, increased self-knowledge, self-esteem, and acceptance of responsibility for behavior and learning.

"We address ourselves to both the academic and emotional needs of our students, for many times the learning disabled child has emotional difficulties. We differ from most public school programs for LH students in the depth and intensity of our programming for academic and behavioral needs."

•**Admission Requirements and Procedure:** 1) Telephone CHILD Center Director. 2) An interview with school psychologist for parent and child. 3) Review of assessments and reports. 4) Visit the school. 5) Six-week trial period upon enrollment.

•**Most Recent Fee Schedule:** Tuition: $37.50 per day; $6,750 for 180 days. Summer Program: $400. Some scholarships are available.

CHILDREN'S CIRCLE CENTER

215A Blackfield Drive (at Via Los Altos), Tiburon, CA 94920
(415) 381-8181

•**Director:** Gudrun Hoy

Children's Circle Center was established in 1976 to serve children aged two and one-half through third grade. There are currently 80 children enrolled and the teacher/student ratio is 1:8 for Preschool and 1:12 for kindergarten through third grade. There are five teachers, all of whom are credentialed. Preschool hours are from 8:30 a.m. to 2:30 p m. Extended day care is available from 7:30 a.m. to 6:00 p.m. at $3.00 per hour. An enrichment program is offered from 3:00 p.m. to 6:00 p.m. at $3.00 per hour. A summer school program is offered.

Accredited by PACE.

•**Philosophy/Goals/Curriculum:** "Children's Circle Center's philosophy is to give the children a positive school experience where their self concept is fostered along with the child's exposure and encouragement towards academic excellence. Children's Circle Center provides a sense of trust by creating an environment that is safe, loving and consistent. It honors the total child academically, cognitively, emotionally, socially, intuitively, creatively and physically, instilling a respect for life, developing in the child a positive self-esteem, and creating and implementing an educational vision for the future. The school feels a total developmental approach towards learning is essential in moving towards physical, emotional, and social independence as well as towards academic progress. The program is based on an integrated curriculum which includes language arts, Spanish, French, reading readiness, reading, writing, mathematics, science, social studies, sensory motor development, drama, arts, gardening, cooking, music, field trips, and computer education."

•**Admission Requirements and Procedure:** After the initial contact, a visit and information session are scheduled followed by an interview and assessment with the child. Admission is as space permits. It is advised to apply by March 31 for kindergarten through grades.

•**Most Recent Fee Schedule:** Tuition: $130 - $440 per month for preschool, depending on the program. Kindergarten through fifth: $365 - $430 per month, depending on the program. The extended day care costs $3.00/hour. Some partial scholarships are available, except for the preschool program. There is a $50 registration fee.

CHRISTIAN LIFE SCHOOL

1370 S. Novato Boulevard (at Rowland), Novato, CA 94947
(415) 892-5713

•**Administrator:** Gregg Mervich

Christian Life School was founded in 1979 and currently serves 320 students, preschool through ninth grade. It is planned to add a high school at a later date. School hours are 8:30 a.m. to 3:00 p.m. Extended day care is available before and after school from 6:30 a.m. to 6:30 p.m. An elementary day care program is offered. There is a dress code. In-school tutoring is available. There is a daily Bible class and chapel once a week. There are 25 teachers on the staff.

Member of the Association of Christian Schools International.

•**Philosophy/Goals/Curriculum:** "Christian Life School offers a quality educational program in a positive social atmosphere. Academic excellence is provided in reading, mathematics, English, Bible, spelling, history and science. Art, music, physical education, and computer literacy are included in the curriculum. Christian Life School provides a service to the community for parents concerned with their children's academic attainment and positive character development. The school strives to instill in each student, with the cooperation of home and church, the moral integrity, spiritual insight and academic ability to live as responsible citizens."

•**Admission Requirements and Procedure:** Notification of testing dates and times will be given upon request to the school office for an application. A personal interview will also be scheduled with the parents, student, and school administration. A copy of the report card from the previous year must be submitted. Parents and students must also agree to the provisions of the Student Handbook. After acceptance, students are expected to abide by the rules and conduct standards of the school.

•**Most Recent Fee Schedule:** Kindergarten: $1,300 per year; elementary: $1,500 per year; junior high (grades seven through nine): $1,500 per year. Registration fee: $40. Book/material fee: $70 (elementary); $80 (junior high). There is a reduction for more than one child enrolled from a family. Limited scholarships are available.

KALEIDOSCOPE SCHOOL

710 Wilson Avenue (at Vineyard), Novato, CA 94947
(415) 897-8761

•**Director:** Marilyn S. Dimond

Kaleidoscope School was founded in 1972 and has a current enrollment of 36 students in preschool through first grade. Average class size is 12 students, and three credentialed teachers are on the staff. Preschool hours are 9:45 a.m. to 12:30 p.m.; kindergarten's, 9:00 a.m. to 12:30 p.m.; and first grade, 9:00 a.m. to 2:00 p.m.

Licensed by the State Department of Social Services and member, Pacific Regional Association of Alternative Schools.

•**Philosophy/Goals/Curriculum:** "Our curriculum is designed to include all phases of a child's development. The academic, creative, social, physical and emotional growth of each child is nurtured in a warm and caring environment. Knowledge and skills are presented through a variety of methods and techniques by skilled teachers who understand children and the processes by which they learn. Highlights in our curriculum include emphasis on reading readiness, reading, math concepts, deductive thinking, artistic and craft projects, story telling, participation with other individuals through group discussion, and games—creative and manipulative. Large muscle control is encouraged through sensory-integration type exercises. The sharing of feelings is encouraged among children and adults."

•**Admission Requirements and Procedure:** We accept children aged three and three-quarter years through seven years. A visit to the school during school hours for the parent, accompanied by the prospective student, is recommended.

•**Most Recent Fee Schedule:** Preschool (three days, either M-W-F or T-Th-F): $1,200 per year; kindergarten (five days): $1,800 per year; first grade (five days): $2,000 per year.

LEEBIL SCHOOL AND LEARNING CENTER

1411 Lincoln Avenue, San Rafael, CA 94901

(415) 454-6618

•**Director:** William Miller

LeeBil School was established in January 1983 to meet the educational, vocational, and developmental needs of secondary aged students in the greater San Francisco Bay Area. Maximum enrollment is 15 students with a 7:1 student-teacher ratio. LeeBil conducts a day program of 180 days and an extended school program of 20 days in the summer. School hours are 9:00 a.m. to 2:40 p.m. daily.

LeeBil is accredited by the State Department of Education and is funded primarily by the supporting school districts who enroll their students in LeeBil.

•**Philosophy/Goals/Curriculum:** Students have a voice in program, discipline, and school operations. One set of guidelines serves both the staff and the student population. Curriculum is designed to meet the public school requirements for graduation. The major goal of LeeBil is to prepare the students for reentry into the public school system where they can interact in the social and academic environment that is necessary for normal young adults.

•**Admission Requirements and Procedure:** Referral of parent by school district, interview with staff and school population, completion of the IEP process.

•**Fee Schedule:** Current tuition is $30 per day or $5,400 for a full year. Local school districts often contract for services.

THE LYCEE FRANCAIS INTERNATIONAL

501 El Camino, Corte Madera, CA 94925

(415) 924-1737

(See also San Francisco Private Schools, page 76)

•**Director:** Pierre Hudelot

The Lycee Francais International is a private, nonprofit school with 350 students in preschool through twelfth grade. Campuses are located in San Francisco and Marin County. The student body is diverse and international, with many students coming from non-French speaking families and arriving at the school with no prior knowledge of French.

The Lycee is backed by the French Government. Academic standards and teacher qualifications are closely monitored by the French Ministry of Education.

•**Philosophy/Goals/Curriculum:** Starting at the preschool level, a judiciously balanced study of both languages and cultures allows children to become rapidly bilingual and to transfer easily from the French to the American system at any time.

The program combines the official French curriculum with a strong English curriculum. Students take the French baccalaureate examination. In addition, those who wish to enter an American college take SAT and Advanced Placement tests. The Lycee's reputation for high academic standards is well established and enables students to enter top universities in the United States and abroad.

The highly qualified French and American teachers are certified by the French Ministry of Education or credentialed by the State of California.

•**Admissions Requirements and Procedure:** There is no deadline for applications. Acceptance is on a first come first served basis. We recommend that applications be sent before Easter to guarantee a space for your child.

•**Most Recent Fee Schedule:** Tuition fees range from $4,000 in kindergarten to $5,550 for tenth through twelfth grades. In addition, a one-time fee of $400 per family is payable upon enrollment. School hours are from 8:30 a.m. to 3:15 p.m. (4:00 p.m. for some high school classes). Extended day care is available to 6:00 p.m.

MARIN ACADEMY

1600 Mission Ave., San Rafael, CA 94901-1859
(415) 453-4550

•**Headmaster:** Bruce Shaw

Established in 1971 as a co-educational, college preparatory day school for students in grades nine through twelve, Marin Academy has a current enrollment of 285 students. With 33 teachers, the average class size is 16, and the student-teacher ratio is 9:1. There is a summer day sports camp offered for children ages eight through thirteen, and a full summer school for both junior and senior high students. A school bus serves students from San Francisco and southern Marin.

Accredited by WASC.

•**Philosophy/Goals/Curriculum:** "The school is committed to strong programs in academics which challenge each student and provide solid preparation for college. Small classes and individual attention enable students to work to the best of their abilities. Each department has courses leading to Advanced Placement and Honors offerings. The school has a broad program in the fine and performing arts and wide opportunities are available in athletics. The school has a well established outdoor education program that includes activities such as backpacking, cross-country skiing, and scuba diving. Recognizing students' needs to be involved with the larger community, Marin Academy has made a significant commitment to community service. As a school, we seek to provide balance in students' lives."

•**Admission Requirements and Procedure:** Applicants are required to take the SSAT and must submit a nonrefundable application fee of $35. All interested students and parents visit the campus for a day. During this visit, candidates will be interviewed by a member of the Admission Committee, and both parents and students visit classes. After a student's final application is received, a transcript of grades and credits is requested in addition to written recommendations from the student's current school.

•**Most Recent Fee Schedule:** Registration Fee: $1,000; Tuition: $7,950 per year; Incidental Fees: approximately $500 per year. Financial aid granted on the basis of need to students who are qualified for the school.

MARIN CATHOLIC HIGH SCHOOL

675 Sir Francis Drake Boulevard, Kentfield, CA 94904
(415) 461-8844

•**Principal:** William Isetta

Marin Catholic High School was founded in 1949 and currently serves a student body of 800 students in grades nine through twelve. Class sizes range from 10 to 30 students, with an average class size of 23. There are 45 credentialed teachers and six credentialed counselors on the staff. There is a summer school for remedial students or incoming freshmen in need of additional work to prepare for the coming year. There is a dress code. School hours are 8:30 a.m. to 2:30 p.m.

Accredited by WASC.

• **Philosophy/Goals/Curriculum:** "Students enrolled at Marin Catholic become part of a multifaceted community and, therefore, find themselves bound by responsibilities. They are expected to strive for established goals in the areas of academics, school life, and extra-classroom experiences. Students are required to pursue a course of study which includes four years of English, three to four years of social studies, three and a half to four years of religious studies, two years of mathematics, two years of science, three years of humanities, and one year of physical education. Courses in fine arts, drama, business, and computer science are also offered. Students are also expected to contribute a minimum of 100 hours of community service during their four years in addition to the academic requirements.

"We attempt to meet the needs of our students by providing a Christian atmosphere in which the fullest potential of each individual student may be realized. Because the message of Christ cannot be pursued or lived in a vacuum, the study of religion accompanies work in other disciplines."

• **Admission Requirements and Procedure:** A placement test is given in January for incoming students. Students also need to submit a transcript and recommendations from former teachers. Each student and the student's parents are interviewed by a member of the Marin Catholic staff. Call or write the Admission Office for further details.

• **Most Recent Fee Schedule:** Current tuition: $3,350 plus a registration fee of $400 and a campus fee of $100. Scholarships and job opportunities are available.

MARIN COUNTRY DAY SCHOOL

5221 Paradise Drive, P.O. Box 189, Corte Madera, CA 94925
(415) 924-3743

• **Head of School:** Timothy W. Johnson

Marin Country Day School was founded in 1956 to serve children in grades kindergarten through eighth. There is a current enrollment of 475 students with 51 teachers. Average class size is 16 students. There are three divisions: (kindergarten through two, three through five, six through eight), each with its own director. School hours are 8:20 a.m. to 2:00 p.m. for kindergarten, and 8:20 a.m. to 3:00 p.m. for grades one through eight. A summer school, primarily recreational in nature, is offered. Some tutoring is available. Transportation is provided at extra charge. There is a dress code. Hot lunch provided.

Accredited by CAIS, NAIS.

•**Philosophy/Goals/Curriculum:** "Our purpose is to educate children so that they will achieve the fullest development of their intellectual, social and creative capabilities, and will be equipped to go confidently into secondary education with an enthusiasm for learning and a sense of individual responsibility and personal involvement in society.

"To these ends, the school emphasizes equally a strong academic program and an enriching human environment. The academic program includes thorough content areas and a variety of concurrent options. Art, music and drama are an integral part of the program, as are athletics, team sports and outdoor education."

•**Admission Requirements and Procedure:** Parents are asked to fill out application forms and return them to school as soon as possible after they have visited. Application deadline for kindergarten is January 31; for grades one through eight, February 28.

•**Most Recent Fee Schedule:** Fees range from $5,590 for kindergarten to $6,730 for eighth grade. Tuition includes lunch, books, laboratory, and athletic fees. It does not include transportation. A scholarship program is available.

MARIN HORIZON SCHOOL

330 Golden Hind Passage, Corte Madera, CA 94925
(415) 924-4202

•**Director:** Ann Clark

Marin Horizon School was established in 1977 to serve children two years of age to fourteen years. Current enrollment is 180 children. School hours vary depending on program. Before and after school day care is available for children in primary and elementary classes. There is a summer school program and an active parent group. All teachers are Montessori trained.

Licensed by the State Department of Social Services; member of California Association of Independent Schools and the American Montessori Society.

•**Philosophy/Goals/Curriculum:**

Toddler Program: "At this age, children require a supportive, intimate atmosphere, and a rich environment which encourages refinement of their gross and fine motor movements, develops their social skills of sharing and conversation, and provides avenues for reinforcement of self esteem and confidence."

Primary Program: "The primary class environments are designed to meet the needs of children between the ages of three to five years. These environments are rich in materials which challenge the young child to explore. Our Montessori primary cycle includes the traditional kindergarten year."

Elementary Program: "The elementary academic program is strong in skill development and broad in character. The school emphasizes the values of independence, cooperation, and self-discipline. Education is more than learning factual information; it is the ability to concentrate, to read and write fluently, to research confidently, to complete projects, to work productively, both individually and in a group. It is the capacity to reflect and to value learning.

Middle School Program: "The Middle School is a bridge between the academic foundation to the elementary years and the increased responsibilities of the approaching high school and adult world. It is a time to consolidate social and academic abilities, then extend them to new levels of challenge and understanding." "The ability to make informed choices grows in importance as a child matures. Marin Horizon School is committed to developing this skill in the Middle School program. In their studies, students look behind events to their causes in order to foster critical thinking."

•**Admission Requirements and Procedure:** There are limited school openings. Applications for junior classes must be made by February. Priority is given to siblings and children with a Montessori background.

•**Most Recent Fee Schedule:** Grades one and two: $5,000; Grades three and four: $5,100; Grades five and six: $5,200; Grades seven and eight: $5,400.

MARIN PRIMARY SCHOOL
20 Magnolia Avenue, Larkspur, CA 94939
(415) 924-2608

•**Director:** David Heath

Marin Primary was established in 1975 and currently serves 200 children from preschool through fifth grade. Extended day care is offered from 7:00 a.m. to 7:00 p.m. five days a week, on a twelve-month basis. A full summer school program is offered. Small classes allow an individualized educational approach. Optional lunch and three snacks are provided. Maximum class size is 12 students. There are 30 teachers and a resource specialist on the staff. In addition, there is an ungraded primary classroom for students with moderate learning disabilities.

Accredited by WASC.

•**Philosophy/Goals/Curriculum:** "The Marin Primary program offers a stimulating curriculum that emphasizes the mastery of academic skills and creative expression presented in a humanistic environment that is highly personal. Focus is placed on growth and development of persons in relation to content and subject matter. Thus, curriculum planning attends continuously to the human condition. The school seeks to become a microcosm of a society where responsible interaction is essential. Marin Primary seeks to educate young people so that they will achieve their intellectual, social, and creative capabilities to the fullest potential; and carry into the future an enthusiasm for learning, a sense of responsibility and personal involvement in society. Qualities we want a child to increasingly acquire include positive self concept, self discipline, caring for the needs of others, flexibility in response to challenge and a capacity for wise choice." Enrichment program includes art, music, Spanish, computers, and physical education. There is an extensive afternoon elective program.

•**Admission Requirements and Procedure:** Visiting arrangements and requests for application forms can be made by calling or writing the school.

•**Most Recent Fee Schedule:** Registration fee: $50 per family; tuition fluctuates according to hours per month, from $430 per month to $490 per month.

MARIN SCHOOL FOR LEARNING

P.O. Box 4322
San Rafael, CA 94913
(415) 479-5990

•**Director:** Claire Eckley

Marin School for Learning was established in 1982 to meet the needs of children, ages three through eighteen, preschool through high school, whose language difficulties prevent them from reaching their full academic potential. Maximum class size will be ten to fifteen students. There is a current enrollment of 12 full-time students with a maximum capacity of 24. Staff has Learning Disability Credentials. School hours are 9:00 a.m. to 3:00 p.m. There is a summer program. Adult classes are available.

Registered with the State Department of Education.

• **Philosophy/Goals/Curriculum:** "The Marin School for Learning uses a multisensory method of language instruction. This instruction begins with the smallest unit of sight, sound, and feel (letters), then gradually and systematically proceeds to more complex units of language. This highly structured method emphasizes the development and integration of simultaneous auditory, visual, and kinesthetic associations. Class groupings are homogeneous by academic and social development rather than by fixed grade level."

• **Admission Requirements and Procedure:** Each prospective student is evaluated to determine that the basic problem is one of language difficulty, that the student is of average or above average intelligence, and that there are not primary emotional problems which would prevent successful learning experience. The following procedures are followed: A screening test of language difficulty, evaluation of individual I.Q. test scores, Wide Range Achievement Test, review of past medical and school records recommendations. Further testing if necessary.

• **Most Recent Fee Schedule:** Tuition: $500 per month. Scholarship and tuition aid available.

MARIN WALDORF SCHOOL

755 Idylberry Road, San Rafael, CA 94903
(415) 479-8190

• **School Administrator:** Karen Rivers

Marin Waldorf School was established in 1972 and is located on a ten-acre campus in Marinwood. There are currently 165 students enrolled in kindergarten through eighth grade. Average class size is 20 students. Teachers are specially trained in the Waldorf method. School hours are 8:30 a.m. to 3:00 p.m. (Kindergarten 8:30 a.m. to 1:00 p.m.).

Accredited by Association of Waldorf Schools of North America.

• **Philosophy/Goals/Curriculum:** "Waldorf education cultivates a heartfelt joy for learning and an open-minded wonder of the unfolding experience of the world. We offer a comprehensive academic program which is inseparably interwoven with the artistic, cultural and social life. All of the subjects in the curriculum weave a tapestry whose theme is the striving of humankind. Beginning at the kindergarten level, an understanding of life evolves in which science, art and the history of human evolution find integral relationships to one another.

A child entering the Marin Waldorf School is met with creative, challenging experiences which awaken the intellect and nurture the heart. The values of reverence and respect for all life are cultivated in each child. Through wonder, gratitude and love, seeds are sown which mature into responsible, conscious deeds. This framework of understanding empowers students with a trust for inner truth, a sense of reverence and responsibility for our planet Earth, and a commitment to the future of our world."

•**Admission Requirements and Procedure:** Requests for information and application forms can be made by calling the school.

•**Most Recent Fee Schedule:** Application fee: $25 per child; Tuition (paid annually, semi-annually, or monthly): kindergarten: $4,100; Grades one through five: $4,400; Grades six through eight: $4,950. (There is a $20 set-up fee if tuition is paid monthly.)

MOUNT TAMALPAIS SCHOOL

100 Harvard Avenue (at California), Mill Valley, CA 94941
(415) 383-9434

•**Director:** Dr. Kathleen Mecca

Mount Tamalpais School was founded by Dr. Mecca in 1976. The school is located on ten acres in Marin County. There are currently 240 students enrolled in kindergarten through eighth grade. Average class size is 24 to 32 students, with a student-teacher ratio of 12:1. There are 25 credentialed teachers on the staff. School hours are 8:15 a.m. - 12:15 p.m. for kindergarten children and 8:15 a.m. - 3:15 p.m. for grades one through eight. Extended day care is available from 3:15 p.m. - 6:00 p.m. Bus service is available. Uniforms are required.

Accredited by CAIS, WASC, NAIS.

•**Philosophy/Goals/Curriculum:** "The school's purpose is to provide students with a solid academic foundation which will generate an enthusiasm for learning. The departmentalized curriculum in grades one through eight allows each teacher to use a variety of teaching methods to strengthen individual skills. This individual instruction maximizes the inherent potential of each student and fosters a respect for each student's special interests and abilities. The school curriculum is strongly academic and focuses on a thorough understanding of concepts and research skills while also providing a balanced program. Subjects include reading, language arts, math, literature, art and art history, Spanish, French, Latin, science, social science, computer science, physical education, music, and health."

•**Admission Requirements and Procedure:** Interested parents are asked to visit the school before completing an application. There is a $50 application fee. All students applying for kindergarten through eighth grades are tested. Application includes references and information about the child's social, emotional, and academic development. Application deadline for kindergarten is February 1; for grades one through eight deadline is March 1. Notification of acceptance is given mid-March.

•**Most Recent Fee Schedule:** 1989 - 1990 Tuition: kindergarten: $4,750; grades one through eight: $5,550 per year. Financial assistance is available and is determined on the basis of merit and financial need.

NORTH BAY MARIN SCHOOL

80 Lomita Drive, Mill Valley, CA 94941
(415) 381-3003

•**Directors:** Richard Curley & Cheryl Hummel

The North Bay Marin School is a private community school established in 1979, serving grades six through twelve. There are currently 90 students and 12 teachers. School hours are 8:45 a.m. to 3:00 p.m. There is a summer school program.

Accredited by WASC.

•**Philosophy/Goals/Curriculum:** "Our interest is in creating a quality school which meets the needs of parents and students alike, while providing a positive environment in which to learn. We feel that it is the relationship between the students and the teacher, as well as joint communication with the parent or guardian, that makes the difference between a mediocre school and an excellent one. NBMS is an academically oriented school that has an overall goal that each student be a success, both academically and behaviorally. It is the task of the school to encourage and secure self-management and self-esteem in each student so that he may assume responsibility for himself.

"NBMS offers all courses necessary for college preparation. NBMS offers both a standard diploma for graduation and a college preparatory diploma for college bound or honor students."

•**Admission Requirements and Procedure:** NBMS does not require an entrance examination of its students; however, a basic achievement test is given after enrollment for the purpose of placement. An in-depth interview with one of the directors is required before enrollment along with teacher recommendations and a student essay.

•**Most Recent Fee Schedule:** Tuition: $5,000 per year. Some scholarship funds are available.

OPEN DOOR CHRISTIAN SCHOOL

720 Diablo Avenue, Novato, CA 94947
(415) 892-6044
Mailing Address: P.O. Box 1980, Novato, CA 94948

•**Administrator:** Sherman Moyer
•**Director:** Louise Ross

Open Door Christian School was established in 1979 and currently serves preschool through grade six. Average class size is limited to 16 in kindergarten and 22 in first through sixth grades. The staff have California teaching credentials. Extended day care for preschool and kindergarten is offered. Art, music, science, and physical education are offered to all students. Open Door Christian School is affiliated with the Association of Christian Schools International.

•**Philosophy/Goals/Curriculum:** "Open Door Christian School is non-sectarian and non-denominational. Our purpose is to provide the best of Christian training and educational teaching to our students. Our staff are committed to meeting the children's needs whether spiritual, emotional, physical, or educational, and to pray for and act in such a way that those needs are met. Each day begins with singing, prayer and a Bible story or lesson. Computers are used in classes. Children are encouraged to work at their own pace and an individualized instructional approach is utilized. The Learning Center offers an individualized testing and tutoring program designed to improve students' learning abilities. Students eagerly attend the sessions and respond by rapidly increasing their skills and abilities."

• **Admission Requirements and Procedure:** There is an application for completion by the parent. Administrator, child, and parent have a conference and visit a
classroom. Academic testing is done at all levels to determine placement.

• **Most Recent Fee Schedule:** Pre-kindergarten (M-W-F, 8:30 a.m. to 11:30
a.m.): $105 per month; two and one-half to three year olds (T-Th, 8:30 a.m. to
11:30 a.m.): $85 per month. Kindergarten: $130 per month; grades one through
six: $150 per month. Registration and materials: $150 per year. Reductions are
available for siblings.

REAL SCHOOL

50 El Camino Drive, Corte Madera CA 94925
(415) 927-0249

• **Director:** Mary Refrem

Founded in 1986, Real School reflects a method of education developed by
American philosopher and educator, L. Ron Hubbard. Present enrollment is 28,
grades kindergarten through eight. There are three full-time and three part-time
teachers, trained in observing and correcting learning barriers. Average class size
is nine students. School hours are 9:00 a.m. to 3:00 p.m. Extended day care hours
are 8:00 a.m. to 9:00 a.m. and 3:00 p.m. to 6:00 p.m. There is a summer program
including academics, arts and crafts, and field trips. A neat and clean appearance
is required.

Registered with the State of California.

• **Philosophy/Goals/Curriculum:** "Real School is a unique, non-profit school.
We utilize the highly successful method of education developed by L. Ron
Hubbard, American philosopher and educator. Our students learn how to study
and how to apply what they have learned in a safe, drug-free environment; and our
teachers are trained to recognize and correct potential learning barriers. Rather
than assigning grades, Real School requires its students to demonstrate 100
percent mastery of all subjects, beginning with the basics.

"While our curriculum lays a foundation for a technical world, we recognize the
importance of creativity. Art and music are an integral part of our standards,
providing a balance with the academics, computers and manual skills. We offer an
extensive physical education program, as well, that builds improved motor skills,
strength and good physical health.

"Real School also emphasizes the practical principals involved in being responsible as a group member, and knowing about and caring for oneself, family and community. We teach a child how to communicate, how to listen, and the value of honesty. The high personal, academic and artistic standards at Real School ensure a quality education for your child."

• **Admissions Requirements and Procedure:** Enrollment is continuous throughout the year. Standard health requirements for school age children are applicable. Parents agree to abide by the terms of the contract with the school.

• **Most Recent Fee Schedule:** Twelve-month schedule: $373 per month; ten-month schedule: $406 per month. Summer fees differ from September to June tuition. There are no scholarships available at this time.

ST. ANSELM'S SCHOOL

40 Belle Avenue, San Anselmo, CA 94960-2892
(415) 454-8667

• **Director:** Odile Gaudreau Steel

St. Anselm's was founded in 1924 and serves children in kindergarten through eighth grade. It has a current enrollment of 150 students with ten teachers. Average class size is 20 students. There is an extended day care program from 7:00 a.m. to 6:00 p.m. Uniforms are required.

Accredited by WCEA and WASC.

• **Philosophy/Goals/Curriculum:** "As a parochial school of the Archdiocese of San Francisco, St. Anselm's purpose is to form students in Christian living through a curriculum integrated with the teachings of Christ and Gospel values, administered by a dedicated and professional staff of Christian men and women. We offer a strong academic curriculum with several co-curricular programs geared to the average and above students. We do not have facilities or staff to offer a wide range of special education programs."

• **Admission Requirements and Procedure:** Parents should submit baptismal certificates (if applicable) and child's last report card. Transferring students must have average grades or better in academic subjects. Conduct grades must be average or better. New students are required to submit a recommendation from their current teacher. Final approval rests with the principal. Kindergarten registration should be completed by mid-February. New student registrations completed by March.

•**Most Recent Fee Schedule:** Fees are based on a ten-month schedule. Kindergarten: $144 per month; grades one through eight: one child/$187.50 per month; two children/$324.50 per month; three children/$434 per month. Special rates apply if tuition is paid annually or semi-annually. Nonrefundable registration/supply fee per child: kindergarten-fifth grade/$140; grades six through eight/$160. Parents are asked to volunteer 50 hours of time at $7.00 per hour or $350 per year. Single-parent families are asked to volunteer 25 hours or $175 per year.

ST. HILARY SCHOOL

765 Hilary Drive (Tiburon Blvd. and Rock Hill Drive), Tiburon, CA 94920
(415) 435-2224

•**Principal:** Mary Ahlbach

St. Hilary School was founded in 1963 and has a current enrollment of 243 students in kindergarten through eighth grade with 14 credentialed teachers. Average class size is 25 students. School hours are 8:10 a.m. to 2:30 p.m. There is a summer school program. Golden Gate Transit runs a special bus to the playground area. Uniforms are required. Day care to 6:00 p.m.

Accredited by WASC and WCEA.

•**Admission Requirements and Procedure:** Both an interview and a placement test are conducted. Notification of accceptance takes place in April.

•**Most Recent Fee Schedule:** Tuition is $1,860 per year, or $170 per month. Financial aid is available, limited to partial assistance.

ST. MARK'S SCHOOL

375 Blackstone Drive (at Las Gallinas), San Rafael, CA 94903
(415) 472-7911

•**Headmaster:** Damon Kerby
•**Director of Admissions:** Jo-Ann Simpson

St. Mark's is a coeducational school established in 1980 and currently serving 315 students in kindergarten through eighth grade. School hours are 8:45 a.m. to 2:30 p.m. for kindergarten and 8:45 a.m. to 3:15 p.m. for grades one through eight. Extended day care is available until 6:00 p.m. A summer school is offered which is a combination of academic and enrichment activities. Average class size is 21 students. There are 34 teachers. St. Mark's has an active parent group and there is a dress code.

Fully accredited by WASC, NAIS, and CAIS.

•**Philosophy/Goals/Curriculum:** "The objective of the program is to master the basic academic subjects, thus setting a firm foundation for a well-rounded education. The development of strong study habits, good citizenship, and an appreciation of our American heritage is essential in reaching this objective. Basic curriculum for grades one through eight includes reading, phonics, vocabulary, English grammar, composition, penmanship, spelling, mathematics, history, geography, and sex education as appropriate. Art, music, foreign languages, physical education, computer education, drama, and science are taught by specialists."

•**Admission Requirements and Procedure:** Candidates return the application form and application fee to the office no later than March 1 for the following September. Candidates will spend time at the school. Kindergarten candidates will have an interview, and candidates for grades one through eight will be tested. Appointments to observe must be made in advance. St. Mark's agrees to common notification dates with other Independent Schools in the Bay Area.

•**Most Recent Fee Schedule:** Fees range from $4,275 per year for kindergarten to $5,250 for eighth grade. Books are in addition to tuition. Tuition may be paid in one, two, or four installments. Some scholarship aid is available.

ST. RAPHAEL'S SCHOOL

1100 Fifth Avenue, San Rafael, CA 94901
(415) 454-4455

•**Director:** Monsignor Thomas Kennedy

St. Raphael's School was founded in 1889 and is located in the Mission San Rafael on A Street. 250 students are enrolled in grades kindergarten through eighth. Average class size is 30 to 35 students with 11 full-time, fully credentialed teachers and four part-time teachers.

Accredited by WASC.

•**Philosophy/Goals/Curriculum:** "As a faculty we believe that the parents are the primary educators and we are here to assist them in their task. As their partners in education we recognize the need for mutual consideration and support. We believe as a gospel people that our primary challenge is to present the gospel message of Jesus, to develop a Christian community and to encourage a spirit of service to others.

"We commit ourselves to providing a flexible and stimulating classroom environment wherein each student will develop his or her intellectual capabilities and will develop growth in factual knowledge, critical thinking, intellectual curiosity and innate creativity. We believe people must learn to live together in respect, peace and love on personal, group, national, and world levels. We believe that developing and maintaining healthy bodies is critical to full development religiously, intellectually, and socially."

•**Admission Requirements and Procedure:** Registration of students in the school takes place in April. Registration is then open to all students on a space-available basis.

•**Most Recent Fee Schedule:** Registration fee: $115. Tuition: $1,400 in parish; $1,600 out of parish. Fees are subject to change on a yearly basis. Summer school and extended day care are also offered. Financial aid is available.

ST. RITA SCHOOL

102 Marinda Drive (at Sir Francis Drake), Fairfax, CA 94930
(415) 456-1003

•**Principal:** Maureen Cassidy

Founded in 1957, St. Rita School has a present enrollment of 210 students in grades kindergarten through eighth with six full-time and five part-time teachers, all credentialed, having either BA or MA degrees. Average class size is 23 students. School hours are 8:25 a.m. to 3:00 p.m. Extended day care hours are available at $2.50 per hour for one child and $3.50 for two or more children from 7:15 a.m. to 8:00 a.m. and from noon to 6:00 p.m. Uniforms are required.

Accredited by WASC and WCEA.

•**Philosophy/Goals/Curriculum:** "We believe that when all the learning theories are distilled, the most important asset a school can provide each of its students is a positive self-image. We work hard to build an environment that is based on encouragement and reward. We place a tremendous emphasis on communication among parents, faculty, administration, and students. We seek to make a difference in the lives of our students by providing the skills, study habits, and appreciation for knowledge that will allow them to successfully pursue higher learning and, ultimately, career goals they set.

"The school's academic format consists of classroom instruction for six and one-half hours per day , and nightly homework ranging from 20 minutes for first graders to 60 - 90 minutes for eighth graders. Our objective is to challenge students to perform at the peak of their abilities. All classes are tested at least once each year against a nationwide peer group.

"St. Rita's makes extensive use of teachers' aides and parent volunteers in the classroom. This approach is particularly helpful to children having specific learning difficulties that can be improved through repetition."

• **Admission Requirements and Procedure:** The school secretary will arrange an interview and school tour with the principal. Prospective kindergartners will be interviewed and given some basic testing by the kindergarten teacher. Call the school office for a registration packet outlining the requirements. Year-round application is available.

• **Most Recent Fee Schedule:** There is a $150 registration fee per student. Kindergarten tuition: $1,250; grades one through eight: $1,650. With two children: $2,550 per year. With three or more children: $2,900. Payments are spread over 12 months. Financial aid is available based on need.

SAN DOMENICO EARLY EDUCATION SCHOOL

1500 Butterfield Road, San Anselmo, CA 94960

(415) 454-0200

• **Principal/Director:** Carol Chase

Founded in 1973, San Domenico Early Education School has a present enrollment of 70 students aged four to seven, pre-kindergarten and kindergarten. There are five full-time and two part-time teachers, for a teacher-student ratio of 1:12. The teachers are credentialed, having five or more years' experience. School hours are 8:15 a.m. to 12:15 p.m. Extended day care is available from noon to 3:00 p.m. at $4.00 per hour. Care for kindergartners is available from 3:00 p.m. to 6:00 p.m. also. There is no summer session. Uniforms are required.

• **Philosophy/Goals/Curriculum:** "The philosophy of San Domenico Early Education School is one that is based on an equal regard for the individual child's emotional, social, physical and intellectual growth. The developmentally sequenced curriculum provides opportunities for success and growth in each of the four areas using a multi-sensory, "hands-on" approach. Learning activities capitalize on the child's inborn desire to investigate, explore and interact with the environment. The emphasis of the program is on learning to learn and includes goals involving thinking, reasoning, expressing ideas and learning to manipulate symbols."

•**Admission Requirements and Procedure:** The child must be developmentally age four by December 1. We recommend completion of a preliminary application at least two years prior to the year of entrance. Both parent and child are scheduled to visit the school the year preceding admission. Acceptance notification is in April.

•**Most Recent Fee Schedule:** Tuition may be paid annually, semi-annually, quarterly, or monthly. Tuition is $2,000 for three mornings pre-kindergarten and $3,100 for five mornings pre-kindergarten and kindergarten programs. A limited amount of financial aid is available.

SAN DOMENICO LOWER SCHOOL

1500 Butterfield Road (off Sir Francis Drake), San Anselmo, CA 94960
(415) 454-0200

•**Principal:** Susan A. Maino

Founded in 1859, San Domenico Lower School is a Roman Catholic coeducational school. Enrollment is presently 177 in grades one through eight. The large campus is on 550 acres, including classrooms, library, science laboratory, computer, art and science building, swimming pool, music pavilion, tennis courts, and stables. There are 17 full-time and four part-time teachers, with an average of 11 years' experience. Class size averages 20 to 25 students. School hours are 8:30 a.m. to 3:30 p.m. Extended day care is also available at $30/week.

Accredited by WASC and CAIS.

•**Philosophy/Goals/Curriculum:** "San Domenico, an independent Catholic school, embraces the Dominican tradition of the pursuit of truth. We believe that the heart of the school experience is the development of each student's unique sense of self. We strive to help our students grow from childhood to responsible adulthood according to their individual capabilities, aspirations and needs.

Recognizing the family as the primary educator, we seek to foster the partnership of parents and teachers in all facets of this development: intellectual, spiritual, artistic, social, emotional and physical. We challenge our students academically, guide them in study, and provide opportunities for them to apply their knowledge and skills in a creative manner. We help them to develop spiritual and moral values, to deepen their faith in and love for God, and to exemplify these values in their daily living. We assist them in developing their musical, artistic and athletic talents, and provide opportunities for them to share these with others. We seek to foster a strong sense of citizenship and social justice by cultivating virtues of responsibility, cooperation, and leadership. We encourage our students to under-stand and appreciate people of diverse cultural, religious and ethnic backgrounds. We work toward these goals within a Christian atmosphere of care, concern and mutual trust.

"Along with instruction in the areas of religion, English, reading and literature, spelling, handwriting, mathematics, science/health/safety, and library skills, the curriculum features French, Spanish, art, music, computers, library science, physical education, swimming, tennis and horseback riding.

"Extracurricular activities include Athenian/Spartan rallies, Christmas and Spring performances, and field trips. After-school activities include sports, language workshops, choir, yearbook, homework workshops, library, math and economics teams, private music and art instruction, as well as scouting.

"San Domenico Lower School is divided into three sections: Primary (grades one through three), Middle Level (grades four through five), and Junior High (grades six through eight), in order to address the unique needs of students at various stages of development. Teachers of each section meet regularly to discuss and evaluate their students' progress. While focusing on the stages of develop-ment of each student, we also encourage and promote interaction through the grades by our counselor/charge program, school team activities, and Student Council."

•**Admission Requirements and Procedure:** The school encourages a visit to the campus on visiting days, or on tours arranged by appointment. Interested students are encouraged to experience a day with potential classmates. There is an applica-tion to be submitted with a testing fee for an entrance exam which measures present achievement and potential for continued learning. A general admissions test date is scheduled for February; other dates are set throughout the year through

August. The school adheres to a policy of rolling admissions. Academic records and recommendations from a student's current school are also used as part of the evaluation process.

•**Most Recent Fee Schedule:** Tuition may be paid yearly, bi-annually, or monthly with interest. Tuition is $4,650 per year. Activity fee: $75. Book costs: $120.

SAN DOMENICO HIGH SCHOOL

1500 Butterfield Road, San Anselmo, CA 94960
(415) 454-0200

•**Principal:** Sister M. Gervaise Valpey, O.P.

"San Domenico High School, established in 1850, is a Catholic, college preparatory boarding and day school for girls in grades nine through twelve. The campus is nestled in the midst of 550 acres, which serve as a natural laboratory. In addition to its strong academic program, San Domenico offers a nationally recognized conservatory music program." Current enrollment is 150 students, with a faculty of 25 credentialed teachers. Average class size is ten students. Uniforms are required. Bus transportation is available.

Accredited by WASC and CAIS.

•**Philosophy/Goals/Curriculum:** "As a college preparatory school, San Domenico's curriculum offers students the opportunity to prepare for the requirement of colleges and universities throughout the United States. Recognizing the many talents and individual differences in students has led to diversity and choice in course offerings. Students may also elect to follow a performing arts or visual arts curriculum. The standard program includes four years of social studies, two to three years of science, three to four years of foreign language, four years of religious studies, a semester of computer science, keyboarding, as well as courses in music, art, physical education, and drama. Some of the serious language students may qualify for a student exchange study program. A full program of athletics including basketball, volleyball, swimming, tennis, horseback riding, track, and soccer is offered. All students are required to give 100 hours of community service prior to graduation."

•**Admission Requirements and Procedure:** Students are admitted to San Domenico on the basis of their past grades, recommendations, test (SSAT) scores,

and their desire and ability to do college preparatory work. An interview and visit
to the campus are required.

•**Most Recent Fee Schedule:** Tuition for day students is $7,560, and for residents, $14,500. The tuition includes lunch for all students; books and supplies are
extra. The student activity fee is $200, and resident activity fee is $225. Financial
aid is available.

SKY'S THE LIMIT

2950 Kerner Boulevard, San Rafael, California 94901
(415) 457-1550

•**Director:** Soula Dontchos

Sky's the Limit school was established in 1987 to provide an innovative,
comprehensive, and highly effective program for children with special needs and
their families. Each classroom has five to seven students with a team of two or
three staff responsible for each class. School hours are 9:00 a.m. to 2:15 p.m.
Sky's the Limit is an eleven-month program. No extended day care is provided.
The school serves 20 children, ages six through fourteen.

•**Philosophy/Goals/Curriculum:** "Interwoven in the curriculum of reading,
spelling, mathematics, computers, science, geography and social studies is a broad
spectrum of special services available to all students and implemented on the basis
of individual readiness and need. These services include speech and language
therapy, movement therapy, physical therapy and music instruction, Feldenkrais
work, yoga, tai chi, life skills preparation, problem-solving and activity groups, prevocational skills preparation, Slingerland lessons and art.

"A special feature of the program is the daily opportunity for remediation and
enhancement of the sensory and neuromuscular systems necessary for the complex
process of learning. In addition, after the initial observation period, attention will
be directed, when deemed appropriate, toward determining possible biochemical
imbalances which might interfere with optimal functioning.

"Family work is an integral part of the program as the impact on the family of
the child with multiple needs is strongly felt. A range of services is available and
adapted to the life style and preferences of each family."

•**Admission Requirements and Procedures:** At the time of enrollment, a
multidisciplinary team evaluates each youngster and formulates an individualized,

educational-therapeutic, prescriptive plan with methodology tailored to each student's developmental needs and learning style.
•**Most Recent Fee Schedule:** Call for tuition information.

SPARROW CREEK MONTESSORI SCHOOL
304 Caledonia Street (between Locust and Litho), Sausalito, CA 94965
(415) 332-9595

•**Head of School:** Judith Bang-Kolb
Sparrow Creek is a Montessori school founded in 1974. Current enrollment is 22 students from two and one-half to six years of age, with two full-time teachers and one part-time, with Montessori credentials and experience in this type of school. Average class size is 22. School hours are from 8:30 a.m. to 2:45 p.m. Extended day care hours are 7:00 a.m. to 8:30 a.m. and 2:45 p.m. to 6:00 p.m. Summer sessions are available.
•**Admissions Requirements and Procedure:** Students are accepted on a first-come, first-served basis.
•**Most Recent Fee Schedule:** Tuition is $280 per month. Financial aid is available based on need.

SUNNY HILLS CHILDREN'S SERVICES
(aka **JAMES R. SYLLA SCHOOL**)
300 Sunny Hills Drive, San Anselmo, CA 94960
(415) 457-3200

•**Executive Director:** Robert McCallie
•**Program Director:** Pollie Gassler, M.S.
Sunny Hills provides intensive treatment for youngsters with serious emotional and educational problems. The agency offers a day program and residential treatment serving 40 students, coed, ages 13 through 18. The residential school is for educationally handicapped youngsters. All teachers have special education credentials. A large vocational training center, staffed by school faculty, adjoins the school building. The school staff includes the principal, a consulting psychologist, three credentialed classroom teachers, a speech therapist, a reading specialist, a Title I tutor, and three instructional aides. It is a year-round program

including a six-week summer school. Average class size is 13 students.

Licensed by the State Department of Social Services and registered with the State Department of Education. Certified by the California State Department of Special Education. Accredited by JCAHO.

•**Philosophy/Goals/Curriculum:** The objective of Sunny Hills "is to develop the self-understanding, self-control, and tools learning youngsters need to function successfully in their community, at their schools and with their family and friends. The residential program is a structured therapeutic community including highly individualized educational plans, individualized programs of therapy, occupational therapy and vocational training, family therapy and continued medical and psychiatric evaluation."

•**Admission Requirements and Procedure:** Youngsters are admitted to the residential program after a thorough medical, psychiatric, and academic evaluation. Referrals are generally made by community agencies, physicians, or parents. Severely retarded youngsters are not accepted.

•**Most Recent Fee Schedule:** Residential Treatment: $197 per day; school: $107 per school day, paid by parents, Department of Social Services, Mental Health, private hospitalization insurance, and State Department of Education.

TAM CREEK SCHOOL

50 El Camino Drive, Corte Madera CA 94965
(415) 927-3336

•**Director:** Joyce Hodgkinson

Tam Creek School was founded in 1979 and has a current enrollment of 50 students from junior kindergarten to fifth grade. The four full-time and three part-time teachers are credentialed and average ten years' experience. Class size averages 12. School hours are 9:00 a.m. to 3:00 p.m. Extended day care is available from 7:30 a.m. to 9:00 a.m. and 3:00 p.m. to 6:00 p.m. at an additional cost of $2.25 per hour. There is a summer camp that includes hikes, nature classes, and an olympics. There is no dress code.

Accredited by CAIS.

•**Philosophy/Goals/Curriculum:** "Tam Creek School was founded in 1979 in Mill Valley. The founders created a school based on the concept that learning is an exciting, creative experience. This is a place where children can learn in a nurturing environment with classes small enough to actively participate in the learning process. Tam Creek students are encouraged to be 'at home in the world'. They frequently interact with local, state and national officials about their concerns for the future of their planet.

"Our classes are small: 15 students or less. This permits very close interaction between teacher and student. Studies have found that the amount of time spent interacting with a teacher has a positive effect on self-esteem, as well as encouraging 100 percent understanding of a subject.

"We keep parents informed of their children's progress. Folders of school work are sent home every two to three weeks in the lower grades. Parent conferences occur twice yearly; additional conferences are scheduled during the school year as the need arises.

"We encourage parents to help out by assisting in the classroom, driving on field trips, helping at work days, and planning parties and functions.

"We stress the basics: reading, writing and arithmetic. Students are encouraged to discover concepts and to think and express themselves clearly. We teach critical thinking skills and encourage students to apply new ideas to real life situations. We offer piano, violin and recorder lessons twice weekly in a Suzuki music program. We offer Spanish, Art, Drama, and Physical Education to all students as part of the basic curriculum. IBM's 'Writing to Read' program – a computerized writing/reading program – is part of our kindergarten-first grade curriculum."

•**Admission Requirements and Procedure:** Private tours are scheduled by appointment. You will have time to spend in the classroom, to meet and talk with prospective teachers, and to meet the director. All prospective students spend a day in the classroom. During that time, every effort is made to expose the student to a typical school day. Appropriate skills are also tested. Applications deadline is March 15; after this date, they will be considered if space is available, with notification of acceptance by March 22. Financial aid is offered based on need.

•**Most Recent Fee Schedule:** Tuition for the junior kindergarten is $2,800 per year; $295 monthly. Tuition for kindergarten to fifth grade is $3,600 yearly and $375 per month. There is a $120 fee for materials, insurance and testing and a $75 application fee. Music fee: $250 per year or $25 per month, and Spring Camp (fourth to fifth grades) is approximately $110. There is a 10 percent sibling discount.

TIMOTHY MURPHY SCHOOL
Box M, San Rafael, CA 94913
(415) 499-7616

•**Director:** Marjorie Crump-Shears

Timothy Murphy School (TMS) is a day program which serves boys between the ages of seven to fourteen who are residents at St. Vincent's School for Boys in San Rafael. The students at TMS have one or both of the following: severe emotional disturbances, significant learning disabilities. All have serious psychological and educational problems. Others can be referred for day placement in TMS only.

•**Philosophy/Goals/Curriculum:** "Close collaboration between the residential agency, districts, and the Marin County Office of Education exists so that team planning and program implementation will be most beneficial for each student.

Curricula offered include reading, math, social studies, language arts, physical education, music, art, science, speech and language, movement/drama and, most important, social skills.

Our staff of 26 includes teachers (classroom, full-time, and support, part-time), two counselors, a psychologist, clerical support, instructional aides, a speech/language specialist, nurse, curriculum consultant, and two administrators."

TMS is funded by the California State Department of Education as a non-public school to provide special education services.

•**Admission Requirements and Procedure:** Admission by designation of the IEP (Individual Educational Program) team at any time during the year.

•**Most Recent Fee Schedule:** Free.

Section II
PUBLIC SCHOOLS

Listed by Grade Level Alphabetically

SAN FRANCISCO

MARIN COUNTY

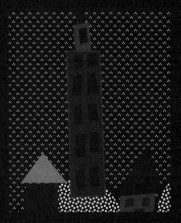

Public Schools SAN FRANCISCO

PUBLIC SCHOOLS: SAN FRANCISCO UNIFIED SCHOOL DISTRICT (S.F.U.S.D.)

135 Van Ness Avenue, San Francisco, CA 94102-5299

(415) 565-9000

• **Superintendent:** Ramon C. Cortines

"The San Francisco Unified School District has 72 elementary schools, grades kindergarten through five; 18 middle schools, grades six through eight; and 23 high schools, grades nine through twelve. The District's unique challenge is to emphasize sensitivity to the varying needs of all students while maintaining a consistent standard of high quality education in every program at every school.

"In addition, schools offer special programs, such as bilingual education, for those who speak limited English or wish to learn a second language. Students with learning, physical, communication, or severe disabilities are served by the District's special education program. Most school sites have gifted and talented (GATE) options for students of high academic or creative potential. Alternative schools also serve special areas of interest and provide options in curriculum and teaching styles."

The above quotation and the paragraph descriptions of individual public elementary, middle, and high schools are taken from *Faces of Education, 1989* with the permission of San Francisco Unified School District, Department of Integration, Public Relations Office; the lengthier descriptions of individual schools were submitted by the respective public schools.

Elementary Schools

ALAMO ELEMENTARY SCHOOL

250 23rd Avenue (between California and Clement Streets), San Francisco, CA
94121 (415) 752-8244

•**Principal:** Dorothy E. Quinones

Alamo is a public elementary school founded in 1926, and located in the
Richmond District. Enrollment is 715 students, kindergarten to fifth grade.
Average class size is 30. Kindergarten hours are from 7:50 a.m. to 11:20 a.m. or
11:25 a.m. to 2:55 p.m. Grade school hours are from 8:15 a.m. to 2:15 p.m.

Alamo was identified as a California Distinguished School.

•**Philosophy/Goals/Curriculum:** "Alamo School strives to recognize and
appreciate the uniqueness of each child while encouraging the development of a
sense of community and responsibility. There is great support for a child's natural
curiosity and creative expression. The learning environment is one of academic
excellence and high expectations. The number one rule at Alamo is 'Be A
Friend.' Special programs are offered in computer instruction, sensory motor,
Junior Great Books Discussion groups, instrumental music, and urban gardening.
The school volunteers program is very active and supports enrichment programs."

•**Admission Requirements and Procedure:** Special tours of the school are given
every Wednesday from 9:00 a.m. to 10:00 a.m. Priority given to students residing
between 17th and 33rd Avenues and between Geary and Lake Streets.

ALVARADO ELEMENTARY SCHOOL

625 Douglas Street (23rd Street and Elizabeth Street), San Francisco, CA 94114
(415) 826-1650

•**Principal:** Rose Barragan

Alvarado Elementary School has been in existence since 1920 and has an enrollment of 400 students from kindergarten to fifth grade. Average class size is 22.

School hours are from 9:00 a.m. to 3:00 p.m., with extended day care for grades two to five. Summer sessions are held with Field Study and an Integrated Curriculum.

•**Philosophy/Goals/Curriculum:** "Alvarado offers a comprehensive instructional program emphasizing a balanced academic and creative arts curriculum in a child-centered environment. It is proud of the positive, warm feeling that is present both in its school and in the three surrounding communities that it serves. Alvarado's curriculum includes: 1) a multi-modal reading and math foundation program for grades K to one, a literature-based program for grades K to five; 2) a well-designed perceptual motor program for grades K to two; 3) a science instruction center with a growing collection of scientific experimentation equipment for grades K to five; 4) a full arts program which includes visual, literary, music and dance components; 5) a comprehensive computer education program focusing on word processing skills, grades K to five.

The after-school arts program provides a continuity of experiences from the day program and is offered to all students. An open door policy for parents is promoted through an active PTA and intensive parent outreach program. Alvarado School is committed to supporting the academic, social, and emotional growth of each student as he/she participates in a racially, ethnically and economically integrated environment." After school Tutorial Program, peer counseling with McAteer High School and family mental health support services are also available.

ARGONNE ALTERNATIVE SCHOOL
675 17th Avenue, San Francisco, CA 94121
(415) 751-6717

"Argonne's school year begins in July, allowing your child to take vacations at his/her convenience, and still fulfill the required minimum of 180 days. At Argonne, students may attend up to 215 days per year. Personalized education, multigraded classes, paraprofessionals, parent participation, enrichment programs, and a strong kindergarten curriculum are provided within a warm and supportive atmosphere."

BESSIE CARMICHAEL SCHOOL
55 Sherman Street, San Francisco CA 94103
(415) 863-2442

Carmichael offers a traditional educational program based upon the sequential development of skills in reading, mathematics, and language arts. Problem-solving activities and critical thinking skills are emphasized in all areas. A positive student self-concept is encouraged and fostered in an atmosphere of stable discipline and caring attention. Part-day preschool enrichment is available.

BRET HARTE SCHOOL
1035 Gilman Avenue, San Francisco, CA 94124
(415) 822-5271

Harte emphasizes the academics with a comprehensive computer program for grades K to five. Our extensive science lab offers hands-on learning for all students. Enrichment is provided through creative and performing arts. Leadership opportunities are available through student council and scouting. Subsidized childcare and part-day preschool are available.

BRYANT SCHOOL
1050 York Street, San Francisco, CA 94110
(415) 647-4959

Bryant provides a rich Spanish bilingual program with a primary emphasis on oral and written communication skills, the fine arts, and multicultural activities. There is an exceptional computer lab that focuses on developing writing skills through use of a word processor. Subsidized childcare is available.

BUENA VISTA ALTERNATIVE SCHOOL
1670 Noe Street, San Francisco, CA 94131
(415) 821-1852

Buena Vista is a Spanish immersion school offering an instructional program in which English-speaking and native-Spanish-speaking students study subject content using Spanish as the language of communication. Parents, students, staff, and community work together to maintain a school atmosphere of concern and respect for children. Private non-profit child care is available.

CABRILLO SCHOOL

735 24th Avenue, San Francisco, CA 94121
(415) 752-9237

Cabrillo provides a multi-ethnic environment with emphasis on a traditional 3 - R program. Additionally, an enthusiastic staff incorporates opera, symphony, live theatre, music, and dance into an enriched curriculum. Computers in classrooms and labs provide every child with hands-on experience.

CLAIRE LILIENTHAL ALTERNATIVE SCHOOL

3950 Sacramento Street, San Francisco, CA 94118
(415) 751-9630

Lilienthal provides a traditional, yet creative, curriculum dedicated to achieving academic excellence in a nurturing environment that is responsive to the needs of the individual child. The basic quality curriculum is enhanced by enrichment activities in music, visual and performing arts, computer literacy and a Science Outdoor School Education Program. Parent commitment and involvement is encouraged. Private non-profit childcare is available.

CLARENDON ALTERNATIVE SCHOOL

500 Clarendon Avenue, San Francisco, CA 94131
(415) 661-0770

Two programs are offered at Clarendon Alternative School: **The Japanese Bilingual Bicultural Program** emphasizes academic achievement in the basic skills areas of reading, writing, and math; Japanese language and culture; multicultural studies; science; art and music. The **Second Community Alternative Program** is a parent-participation community school. The curriculum extends beyond the basics to enriched reading, writing, mathematics, music, and physical education programs. Private non-profit childcare is available.

CLEVELAND SCHOOL

455 Athens Street, San Francisco, CA 94112
(415) 585-0845

Cleveland provides regular education, Spanish bilingual education, and special education for grades K to five. An English as a Second Language program is available. Classroom emphasis is on the basic subjects of reading, math, and language arts. Creative Citizenship is stressed. A strong component of the instructional program is the Children's Theater directed by Dr. Portugal and involving parent participation. Classroom activities in oral language and the performing arts culminate in stage productions twice a year. Participants are children of varied linguistic, academic, and artistic levels.

COMMODORE SLOAT SCHOOL

50 Darien Way, San Francisco, CA 94127
(415) 564-0311

Sloat offers an extensive academic program for all students (including five classes for gifted and talented), as well as supplemental programs in creative arts and music. The staff and programs support and encourage strong parental involvement. Y.M.C.A. -operated childcare is available.

DANIEL WEBSTER SCHOOL

465 Missouri Street, San Francisco, CA 94107
(415) 826-6195

Webster's structured academic program emphasizes the acquisition of oral and written language skills. All curriculum areas include activities that build and support positive self-esteem. The focus is on acceleration, rather than on remediation. Grouping children by ability is being abolished. Classes are moved forward in unison by peer tutoring, cooperative learning, a rich, literature-based curriculum. The goal is every youngster on grade level.

Webster is aiming for strong parent involvement, greater use of community resources, school based management, and increased student expectations.

DR. CHARLES DREW ALTERNATIVE SCHOOL
50 Pomona Avenue, San Francisco, CA 94124
(415) 822-9770

Drew is an alternative school with an early childhood focus, serving students in pre-kindergarten through second grade. The academic program emphasizes active learning and exploration with hands-on materials in a warm, learning environment. Special offerings include a perceptual motor program and interdisciplinary projects. Subsidized child care and part-day preschool enrichment are available.

DOUGLAS TRADITIONAL ALTERNATIVE SCHOOL
4235 - 19th Street, San Francisco, CA 94114
(415) 863-5184

Douglas offers a strong academic program in a well-ordered learning environment. Home-school cooperation is emphasized through our active Parents Club and volunteer program. The curriculum is enhanced by supplemental programs in art and music.

EDISON SCHOOL
3531 - 22nd Street, San Francisco, CA 94114
(415) 821-4510

Edison offers traditional academic programs in the basic subjects, classes in Spanish and ESL and complete media library services. Extracurricular activities include visits to the S.F. Ballet Company and after-school piano classes. Subsidized childcare is available.

EL DORADO SCHOOL
70 Delta Street, San Francisco, CA 94134
(415) 467-6050

El Dorado's students receive instruction in phonics, and the faculty's goal is to include phonics as a part of the whole language approach to teaching Literature Based Reading. Four Star Readers are given special recognition. Awards for academic achievement are given twice a year and a science fair is held annually. After-school childcare is available.

FAIRMOUNT SCHOOL

65 Chenery Street, San Francisco, CA 94131

(415) 285-3828

Fairmount School offers a unique magnet program in marine science with many opportunities for hands-on experiences. This program is interdisciplinary and emphasizes learning in oral and written language, reading, history, geography, and art. A full library program serves the school. K through five bilingual classes in Spanish as well as a third through fifth grade GATE program are also offered.

FILIPINO EDUCATION CENTER

824 Harrison Street (at 4th Street), San Francisco, CA 94107

(415) 543-8430

•**Principal:** Ross Q. Quema

The Filipino Education Center has been in existence since 1972 and serves from 115 - 200 newcomers who are non-English speaking or Limited English Speaking (LEP). Kindergarten through sixth grade children are taught bilingually. Average class size is 15 - 21. School hours are from 8:30 a.m. to 2:30 p.m. Summer school is offered.

•**Philosophy/Goals/Curriculum:** "The Filipino Education Center aims to develop the students' optimum growth in the basic personal, social and academic skills. It aims to respect the pupils' cultural heritage, especially his first language, so that he/she can communicate with others, proceed normally with classroom work and adapt himself to his new environment.

"To meet the District's priority areas and the needs of the Limited English Proficient newcomer students, the FEC provides a year round school calendar . . . that develops listening, speaking, reading and writing skills in English; develops critical thinking skills in subject matter areas through bilingual support; guides pupils to an investigation of the world of math, science and technology around them; prepares them for participation in peer group and community life; develops self confidence and pride in becoming bilingual and bicultural; provides a smooth transition to their new school. In short, the FEC prepares the newcomer pupils for an active and successful participation in an integrated school system."

FRANCIS SCOTT KEY ELEMENTARY SCHOOL

1530 43rd Avenue, San Francisco, CA 94122
(415) 664-2062

Key provides a strong academic program with a variety of teaching strategies that are designed to meet the diverse needs of children. Gifted, Chinese bilingual, and special education classes are part of the school program. Classroom computer programs are in use. Chorus in grades three to five and instrumental music at grades four and five are available.

FRANK McCOPPIN SCHOOL

651 6th Avenue, San Francisco, CA 94118
(415) 752-9825

McCoppin is a traditional school with an emphasis on the 3 - Rs. Also offered are extensive supplemental programs in creative arts and music, enrichment activities including field trips and art classes, and an emphasis on good citizenship and repect for the rights of others. Subsidized childcare is available.

GARFIELD SCHOOL

420 Filbert Street, San Francisco, CA 94133
(415) 982-2823

Garfield provides a structured academic program with emphasis on the traditional 3 - R program. In addition, children are involved in extensive supplemental programs in art, monthly multicultural activities, choral music, and computer education.

GEORGE PEABODY SCHOOL

251 6th Avenue, San Francisco, CA 94118
(415) 565-9574

Peabody is a small, traditional school which offers a structured curriculum for all students integrating the needs of students in GATE, special education, and Limited English Proficiency programs. The Parent/Faculty Organization sponsors a cultural enrichment program that includes visits by resident artists, guest performers, scientists, and opportunities for field trips to the symphony, ballet, and opera.

GEORGE R. MOSCONE SCHOOL
2355 Folsom Street, San Francisco, CA 94110
(415) 647-8526

Moscone's programs are designed to meet the academic needs of our diverse student population. The staff uses all available resources to help students attain their full potential. Parent participation is encouraged and we strive for a teacher-parent partnership. We offer a computer program and all district and federally funded programs.

GEORGE WASHINGTON CARVER SCHOOL
1360 Oakdale Avenue, San Francisco, CA 94124
(415) 822-6391

Carver is a structured academic elementary school that provides a balanced curriculum in an integrated environment. A strong emphasis is placed on oral and written language development and multicultural education. Computers are used as a tool to reinforce reading, math, written language, and critical thinking skills both in a lab setting and individual classrooms.

GLEN PARK SCHOOL
151 Lippard Avenue, San Francisco, CA 94131
(415) 333-6388

"Glen Park School offers a comprehensive curriculum designed to provide a well-rounded experience for all students. Every class schedule includes daily sustained silent reading, circle reading, and computer support. There is weekly library skills instruction. To promote integration in an academically enriched setting the school day is lengthened by 40 minutes. This allows students to continually be regrouped for social interaction while experiencing activities that include language/library/literature classes, computer mini-labs, and performing and visual arts.

Glen Park students are encouraged to develop a positive self-concept, an understanding and appreciation of and repect for others, and a sense of personal and social responsibility. Glen Park students are perceived as the men and women of the twenty-first century. They will be using skills, knowledge, techniques, machines, substances, and methods that are as yet unknown to us. To prepare for this future, Glen Park students must develop: 1) A thirst for knowledge; 2) Different strategies for learning; 3) The basic skills to utilize, store, record, and recall what is known to them; 4) The tools to research what is known to others; 5) The attitudes, behaviors and skills that will help them to live in harmony with themselves, other people, and their environment."

GOLDEN GATE SCHOOL

1601 Turk Street, San Francisco, CA 94115
(415) 931-0449

Golden Gate's major emphasis is placed on the L. A. B. (Language Acquisition Block) program which focuses on reading, oral and written communication, and listening skills. Through the use of additional staff, students are taught in smaller groups according to their skill level needs. The school also publishes an annual anthology of the students' writings and poetry.

GRATTAN SCHOOL

165 Grattan Street, San Francisco, CA 94117
(415) 681-8822

Grattan offers a structured academic program with emphasis on the basics as well as on the arts and sciences, including an extensive Outdoor Education Program. Subsidized childcare and private nonprofit clildcare are both available.

GUADALUPE SCHOOL

859 Prague Street, San Francisco, CA 94112

(415) 334-1975

Guadalupe offers a comprehensive and traditional educational program with a strong emphasis on the basic skills in reading, mathematics, and oral and written language. Other programs focus on the creative and performing arts, critical thinking skills, and computer literacy. Effective school-wide academic and behavioral standards are stressed.

HILLCREST SCHOOL

810 Silver Avenue, San Francisco, CA 94134

(415) 585-3202

Hillcrest emphasizes the 3 - Rs, English as a Second Language, mainstreaming of handicapped children, leadership and citizenship, and opportunities offered through student council activities.

JEAN PARKER SCHOOL

840 Broadway, San Francisco, CA 94133

(415) 421-2988

Parker offers a structured academic program with emphasis on language arts, specifically, oral and written language; choral and instrumental music in grades four and five; Chinese and Spanish bilingual programs; and computer literacy. Students participate in student government as well as other activities that encourage and foster critical thinking, team work, and community service.

JEFFERSON SCHOOL

1725 Irving Street, San Francisco, CA 94122

(415) 664-0342

Jefferson offers an academic program with emphasis on leadership and responsibility. Also stressed are enrichment activities in the performing arts, computer education, and physical education. There is an active P.T.A. program. Subsidized and tuition based childcare are both available.

JOHN MUIR SCHOOL

380 Webster Street, San Francisco, CA 94117

(415) 621-0600

Muir's structured individualized program emphasizes attendance, citizenship, and academic work. Bilingual, English as a Second Language, student improvement, pre-K, after-school tutorial instructional program, and state and federally funded programs are offered.

JOHN SWETT ALTERNATIVE SCHOOL

727 Golden Gate Avenue (between Franklin and Gough), San Francisco, CA 94102

(415)863-6474

•**Principal:** Lois A. Sims

John Swett School was founded in 1911, and opened its doors as an alternative school in 1978. It has 370 students enrolled in pre-kindergarten through fifth grade. Pre-kindergarten is from 7:50 a.m. to 11:05 a.m. and kindergarten is from 7:50 a.m. to 12:40 p.m.; grades one through five are from 7:50 a.m. to 1:50 p.m. Extended care is available until 6:00 p.m. John Swett Alternative School was identified as a California Distinguished School.

•**Philosophy/Goals/Curriculum:** "The diversified program at John Swett Alternative School provides an opportunity for students to learn in an academic environment enriched by a variety of creative experiences. The integrated curriculum focuses on the development of basic skills within a fine arts-multicultural framework. The daily instructional program offers a strong academic approach to the development of basic skills in reading, mathematics, language arts, social studies, and other areas of the elementary curriculum. The students' learning experiences are enriched by regular participation in unique site-developed art, science, and music programs. To enhance the classroom experiences, our program includes professional artists who work with the students on special projects in drama, dance, poetry, painting, and crafts; collaboration with the various museums; field trips; and cultural performances in the school and community. Private classes in Spanish as a foreign language and piano are available to students after school. Instruction in English-as-a-Second Language (ESL) is provided for all students designated as limited and non-English speakers. Parent involvement is a vital part of the program."

JUNIPERO SERRA SCHOOL

625 Holly Park Circle, San Francisco, CA 94110
(415) 285-0252

Junipero Serra offers for children in the neighborhood a program emphasizing strong academics, including Mastery Reading, as well as enrichment activities and student leadership opportunities. There is an active volunteer and parent education program. An on-site after school program is offered by the San Francisco Recreation Department until 5:00 p.m.

LAFAYETTE SCHOOL

4545 Anza Street, San Francisco, CA 94121
(415) 387-3322

Lafayette's academic program is designed to meet the individual needs of its diverse student population. An emphasis is placed on reading, oral and written communication, problem-solving, and critical thinking skills. Students have the opportunity to develop responsibility and skills through participation in a school newspaper, student council, and traffic squad. Parent involvement is encouraged and welcomed.

LAKESHORE ALTERNATIVE SCHOOL

220 Middlefield Drive (at Eucalyptus), San Francisco, CA 94132
(415) 664-6768

•**Principal:** Sharon Guillestegui
Lakeshore School was founded in 1952. It has 560 students from kindergarten through fifth grade. School hours are from 9:20 a.m. to 3:35 p.m. Extended day care is available from 7:45 a.m. to 6:00 p.m. Transportation is provided.

• **Philosophy/Goals/Curriculum:** "Lakeshore Alternative School stresses academic excellence in a supportive learning environment designed to help each child achieve to his/her potential. The staff is also committed to assisting children in learning those human relations skills which contribute to an enjoyable and productive life. The staff's interactions with the children are guided by the basic belief in the dignity of the child as an indivdual.

Supplementary programs provided at Lakeshore Alternative School are an extensive library program supervised by parents five days a week; Perceptual motor program staffed by parents to assist kindergarten through third grade children in learning through the five senses; resident poet/consultant who provides workshops for all students; science lab; computer lab program for all students; an aphasic class that mainstreams into regular classrooms throughout the day; involvement by San Francisco State University to assess learning disabilities and to support and further music, art, and science programs; Lowell High School tutors to assist remedial, average, and advanced students in all academic areas; parent implemented art projects for all students, special multi-cultural activity programs and extended recreational activities; instrumental music classes for upper grade students and a schoolwide performing arts program.

LAWTON ALTERNATIVE SCHOOL

1570 - 31st Avenue, San Francisco, CA 94122
(415) 564-5500

Lawton offers a program devoted to the highest academic and behavioral standards attainable by all students. A traditional program is offered with emphasis placed upon orderly behavior and serious application to academic tasks. Students are taught to know and understand our history, heritage, culture, and governmental structure and to reason in a logical and objective manner. Private non-profit childcare is available.

LEONARD R. FLYNN SCHOOL

3125 Army Street, San Francisco, CA 94110
(415) 648-8727

Flynn offers a program integrating regular education with Spanish bilingual classes, special education classes, and classes for the orthopedically handicapped. Students participate in a variety of extracurricular activities including Boy and Girl Scouts, Glee Club, and an after-school computer club. Subsidized childcare is available.

LONGFELLOW SCHOOL
755 Morse Street, San Francisco, CA 94122
(415) 587-2400

Longfellow emphasizes traditional expectations as they relate to academic achievement, citizenship, enrichment activities, parental/community participation, and discipline.

MARSHALL SCHOOL
1575 - 15th Street, San Francisco, CA 94103
(415) 626-9180

Marshall is a traditional elementary school that stresses oral and written language and basic skills in all subjects. Marshall offers a Spanish bilingual program, and emphasizes good citizenship and the development of a positive self-image. Parent involvement and participation is encouraged.

McKINLEY SCHOOL
1025 - 14th Street, San Francisco, CA 94114
(415) 626-3055

Mc Kinley is a small child-centered magnet school featuring hands-on-science and basic skills. In the classrooms science is woven thematically with other academic subjects. All students are mainstreamed weekly into a science lab, which emphasizes critical thinking skills. Also available: classroom computers, chorus, visual and performing arts, and a yearly junior olympics. Parent participation is encouraged. The unique design of the school provides a rich learning environment.

MIRALOMA SCHOOL

175 Omar Way, San Francisco, CA 94127

(415) 587-4028

Miraloma's traditional academic curriculum is enhanced by programs in computer lab, science lab, physical education (perceptual motor), beginning French, instrumental music, and visual and performing arts. Emphasis is on students' self-esteem with special recognition through the Student of the Week Award program. Private non-profit childcare is available.

MISSION EDUCATION CENTER

2641 - 25th Street, San Francisco, CA 94110

(415) 826-8330

Mission Education Center is a transitional program for the non-English, Spanish-speaking student, aimed at helping the newcomer achieve the necessary skills to succeed. Emphasis is placed on achieving high levels of oral English proficiency and high academic achievement untilizing Spanish as the means of instruction. Students are referred through the school district's Intake Center.

MONROE SCHOOL

260 Madrid Street, San Francisco, CA 94112

(415) 334-0754

Monroe is an academically-oriented school where self-discipline, respect for the rights of others and good manners are stressed. In addition to the regular curriculum, in which language arts and reading are stressed, Monroe offers the service of an ESL/reading resource teacher, special education resource specialist, speech clinician, and instrumental music teacher.

NEW TRADITIONS SCHOOL

1501 O'Farrell Street (between Webster and Hollis), San Francisco, CA 94115

(415) 922-1850

•**Coordinator:** Amy Zins

New Traditions School was started by a group of interested parents in 1976. It is a public alternative school with an enrollment of 120 students, kindergarten through fifth grade. School hours are from 9:30 a.m. to 3:30 p.m.

•**Philosophy/Goals/Curriculum:** "New Traditions School offers: A non-competitive learning environment where all grades cooperatively work together; a rich and extensive natural science environment of plant and animal life; a teaching staff that works closely with the child in small groups using innovative methods of inquiry and problem solving; evaluation of the child's progress based on instructor's observations; an atmosphere fostering self-discipline, self-motivation, creativity, individuality and humanistic awareness. The Teaching Staff offers: Innovative team teaching where each instructor is responsible for each child's learning; a personal curriculum developed by the team instructors to meet the total needs of each child; an instructional atmosphere of respect and mutual trust between the child and the adult; a wealth of training and experience in music, math, reading, creative writing, creative arts, speech, visual arts, dance, drama and exceptional learning instruction." Parents are requested to participate in monthly educational meetings and work days.

PAUL REVERE SCHOOL

555 Thompkins Avenue, San Francisco, CA 94110
(415) 821-7659

Revere's academic program is geared to meet the needs of our diverse multicultural student population, with emphasis on promoting self-esteem. The Media Library, reading labs, computer classes, instrumental music instruction, Conflict Manager Program, and special-funded projects supplement the regular educational program.

RAPHAEL WEILL SCHOOL

1501 O'Farrell Street, San Francisco, CA 94115
(415) 922-0757

Raphael Weill offers a basic academic curriculum that emphasizes academic achievement in a multicultural setting. Teachers and staff have high expectations for students in the areas of listening, following directions, and practicing self-control. Subsidized childcare is available.

REDDING SCHOOL
1421 Pine Street, San Francisco, CA 94109
(415) 673-7931

Redding offers programs serving a student population with diverse cultural and linguistic backgrounds. A strong academic program is provided to meet the learning needs of students and grants from community sources provide for program enrichment. The staff is committed to attaining educational excellence. Subsidized childcare is available.

ROBERT L. STEVENSON SCHOOL
2051 34th Avenue, San Francisco, CA 94116
(415) 564-4159

Stevenson emphasizes a traditional 3 - R program. Chinese bilingual classes are offered for grades K through three; ESL students not in bilingual classes receive ESL instruction or special assistance in LDC (Sheltered English) classrooms. Other alternatives for students include: GATE, a resource specialist program, speech therapy, instrumental music, and school improvement programs. After-school YMCA child care is available.

ROOFTOP ALTERNATIVE SCHOOL
443 Burnett Avenue, San Francisco, CA 94131
(415) 285-1977

Rooftop is a friendly, supportive learning environment which emphasizes student self-worth and self-image in a structured environment. In addition to the core curriculum, Rooftop's program emphasizes the performing and visual arts. Rooftop has a special spirit and sense of community shared by children, staff, and parents. Parent participation is expected. Rooftop was identified as a "California Distinguished School." Parents are invited to call the school for a tour on Observation Day, Wednesdays at 8:15 a.m.

SAN FRANCISCO COMMUNITY ALTERNATIVE SCHOOL
(K-eight)
125 Excelsior Street, San Francisco, CA 94112
(415) 239-1870

•**Principal:** Paul Reinhertz

San Francisco Community Alternative School, founded in 1971, was established by a group of parents who were committed to the philosophy of the cooperative pre-schools. Parents wanted to provide a joyous learning environment in which they would continue to play a visible and essential role. Teachers, students, parents, and the community work together to create an environment in which children learn to develop self-repect; to respect others; to appreciate similarities and differences of all people; to assume responsibility for learning and enjoy the process of learning; and to resolve conflicts by using problem-solving techniques. The interwoven and integrated relationships that all people have to one another in this society and the contributions that all people have made are emphasized. Through the open forum of regular class meetings at all grade levels and supportive student groups, children are enabled to grow and to develop into sensitive, caring indviduals. San Francisco Community School offers a strong academic program that helps children develop critical thinking skills in all curriculum areas. A math and science curriculum from kindergarten through the eighth grade is an integral part of the total curriculum. Individualized instruction, outdoor education, and computer literacy enhance the program.

SANCHEZ SCHOOL
325 Sanchez Street, San Francisco, CA 94114
(415) 626-4527

Sanchez offers a complete spectrum of educational services to meet the needs of a diverse population: GATE, Spanish bilingual, and ESL programs. Other services include a resource specialist, SDC classes (Spanish bilingual day classes), a media librarian, and an elementary student advisor. Students also have the opportunity to participate in a sensory motor program and in choral music. Parent participation is encouraged and childcare is available.

SHERIDAN SCHOOL

431 Capitol Avenue, San Francisco, CA 94112
(415) 586-2200

Sheridan offers a vigorous basic skills program with emphasis on oral and written language, reading, mathematics, and problem-solving skills. Developing the whole child is the focus of classroom activities, team sports, and computer, music, drama and dance programs.

SHERMAN SCHOOL

1651 Union Street, San Francisco, CA 94123
(415) 776-5500

Sherman provides a warm, friendly atmosphere with a program that is student-oriented and conducive to learning. A strong emphasis is placed on an academic curriculum supplemented with enrichment and various educational activities. Sherman was recognized as an outstanding school by the State Department of Education in the 1988 - 89 school year.

SIR FRANCIS DRAKE SCHOOL

350 Harbor Road, San Francisco, CA 94124
(415) 282-8390

Drake provides a structured basic academic program with school-wide emphasis on computers and technology, science and outdoor education, and visual and performing arts within a supportive and culturally sensitive environment. There are innovative programs for parents, including parenting and computer classes. Drake was named a "California Distinguished School" by the State of California.

SPRING VALLEY SCHOOL

1451 Jackson Street, San Francisco, CA 94109
(415) 474-5637

Spring Valley, the oldest school in San Francisco, has a caring staff that provides a challenging, comprehensive, future-oriented curriculum emphasizing science and thinking skills. The curriculum includes programs in Chinese and Spanish bilingual, computers, conflict resolution, multicultural, language and creative arts, and strong parent involvement. Enrichment, such as the artist in residence, is offered through special funding. Spring Valley was chosen to be in a national Thinking Skills Consortium and Science Curriculum Center as well as a "California Distinguished School." The GATE program was nominated for national recognition.

STARR KING SCHOOL
1215 Carolina Street, San Francisco, CA 94107
(415) 282-8615

King offers an academic school program with a strong emphasis on fostering and promoting self-esteem. The special education classes are integrated into the regular program on a daily basis. A full-time librarian and ESL classes add to the curriculum. Sustained Silent Reading is an integral part of the program throughout the school.

SUTRO SCHOOL
235 12th Avenue, San Francisco, CA 94118
(415) 752-4203

Sutro offers a traditional program for all students with emphasis on the language arts and math. GATE, compensatory education, special education, and LEP programs are an integral part of the school's academic picture. LEAP, S.F. Education Fund, and other grants from community sources provide enrichment and enhancement of the core curriculum. Subsidized and tuition-based childcare is available.

ULLOA SCHOOL
2650 42nd Avenue, San Francisco, CA 94116
(415) 564-4240

Ulloa offers a core curriculum of math, reading, and language. Basic skill instruction is integrated into a program that stresses academic achievement and development of positive self-esteem for all students. Instruction incorporates basic skills as well as music, science, social science, fine arts, and physical education.

VISITACION VALLEY SCHOOL

55 Schwerin Street, San Francisco, CA 94134

(415) 239-7396

Visitacion Valley's structured academic program emphasizes the acquisition of oral and written language skills. All curriculum areas include activities that build and support positive self-esteem. Visitacion Valley was identified as a California Distinguished School.

WEST PORTAL SCHOOL

5 Lenox Way, San Francisco, CA 94127

(415) 731-0340

•**Principal:** Jeanne Villafuerte

West Portal School opened its doors in 1926. It has an enrollment of 560 students, kindergarten through fifth grade. Average class size is 30. School hours are from 8:40 a.m. to 2:40 p.m. Extended day care is available all year around (Telephone: 753-1153).

•**Philosophy/Goals/Curriculum:** "West Portal provides a strong, traditional educational program which stresses academic excellence for students through a solid curriculum in basic skills that has been extended to develop scientific and technological literacy through a comprehensive program in science, math, and computers. The staff plans for the instructional needs of students by using a developmental approach to learning which builds upon the acquisition of specific skills and information at each grade level. Reading is key to learning at West Portal. All areas of the curriculum emphasize reading. Students learn math through the Scott Foresman (one through five) and Math Their Way (K through one) programs which focus on the application of mathematical concepts and the mastery of computational skills. A computer lab helps students to acquire computer literacy skills as well as assist them in mastering skills in math and language arts. Science is taught at every grade level. Exploration and discovery underlie the curriculum, and principles are enhanced by field trips."

Other programs offered are the Gifted Program, the Music Program, the Perceptual Motor Program, and the Chinese Immersion Education Program.

WILLIAM R. DE AVILA SCHOOL
1351 Haight Street, San Francisco, CA 94117
(415) 626-0181

De Avila emphasizes language arts acquisition and mastery, improvement of critical thinking skills, and development of an appreciation for multicultural literature and fine arts. Children are given opportunities to make frequent written and oral reports in class and at semi-monthly assemblies. The school's computer lab is used by all classes regularly; each classroom has its own computer. Private non-profit childcare is available.

YICK WO ALTERNATIVE ELEMENTARY SCHOOL
2245 Jones Street (between Lombard and Greenwich), San Francisco, CA 94133
(415) 474-2833

•**Principal:** Shirlene L. Tong
   Yick Wo Alternative Elementary School is located on the eastern slope of Russian Hill adjacent to North Beach and Chinatown. School hours are from 9:30 a.m. to 1:20 p.m. for kindergarten and 9:30 a. m. to 3:30 p.m. for grades one through five. On site childcare is available before and after school by the Embarcadero YMCA.
•**Philosophy/Goals/Curriculum:** "The mission of Yick Wo Elementary School is to develop our students into life-long learners and responsible world citizens. In addition, students learn to appreciate the similarities and differences of all people. The school's curriculum incorporates an interdisciplinary approach to teaching mathematics, social studies, health, art, music, and physical education, with an emphasis on language arts and science. The goal throughout all curriculum areas is to develop students' critical thinking skills, so that students become independent thinkers and doers. The program also aims to maintain a positive learning environment, encouraging each student to develop to his or her fullest potential. Experiences related to classroom learning such as field trips, community resources, audio-visual programs, and multi-cultural activities are an integral part of the total

school program. Homework is assigned four days a week, and parents are required to sign the homework. Parents, friends, and community persons are encouraged to assist and participate in the classroom and other school activities. Interested persons are encouraged to visit Yick Wo School by phoning the school office for an appointment."

Middle Schools

A.P. GIANNINI MIDDLE SCHOOL

3151 Ortega Street, San Francisco, CA 94122

(415) 664-4575

Giannini is a traditional academic middle school with an emphasis on scholastic excellence, while fostering an appreciation and knowledge of the arts and music. Club programs allow for broad student experiences in extracurricular areas.

APTOS MIDDLE SCHOOL

105 Aptos Avenue, San Francisco, CA 94127

(415) 586-6194

In an atmosphere that encourages self-esteem and expands students' horizons, Aptos emphasizes a strong academic program with a variety of electives including foreign languages, science, arts, computer applications, and an extensive performing arts and athletic programs.

BENJAMIN FRANKLIN MIDDLE SCHOOL

1430 Scott Street, San Francisco, CA 94115

(415) 565-9654

Franklin is a hands-on science magnet school that involves all students at all grades. The school programs include GATE; an honors program; a bilingual education/ESL program for Chinese, Vietnamese, and Spanish speaking students; a Reading Demonstration Program; and enrichment programs in computers, band, and chorus, utilizing community resources.

DR. MARTIN LUTHER KING, JR. ALTERNATIVE SCHOOL

350 Girard Street, San Francisco, CA 94134

(415) 468-7290

The enthusiastic and caring staff of MLK provides an outstanding education program emphasizing high academic standards and student achievement. The small size of the school and classes allows for a nurturing environment that assists students in making a successful transition into high school. Students take three years of language arts, math, and science. In addition to the academic core curriculum, students in every grade level have an opportunity to choose from a wide range of electives and experience an extensive outdoor education program.

EVERETT MIDDLE SCHOOL

450 Church Street, San Francisco, CA 94114

(415) 431-0822

Student and parent participation, an outstanding faculty, and individual student recognition characterize Everett's approach to providing a model education. Everett emphasizes variety to meet individual needs and learning styles with frequent, careful monitoring of progress. A full elective program is available featuring music, art, computer science, an ecology program, industrial arts, Spanish, and French.

FRANCISCO MIDDLE SCHOOL

2190 Powell Street, San Francisco CA 94133

(415) 392-8214

The performing arts magnet program at Francisco is designed to create a total school environment that reflects all of the visual and performing arts. Students are able to participate in school activities, clubs, student government, sports, and performing arts productions. Courses offered include drama, theater, orchestra, banking, photography, dance, art, computer graphics, electronics, wood shop, home arts, and yearbook activities.

HERBERT HOOVER MIDDLE SCHOOL

2290 14th Avenue, San Francisco, CA 94116

(415) 564-1226

Hoover is a large, comprehensive middle school with a strong academic base. Performing arts are highlighted by Hoover's award-winning band, orchestra, and chorus.

HORACE MANN ALTERNATIVE SCHOOL

3351 23rd Street, San Francisco, CA 94110

(415) 826-4504

Mann offers a strong academic program in an integrated setting that enables early adolescent students to build a sense of responsibility, confidence, pride in accomplishment, and a positive self-image through academic achievement.

JAMES DENMAN MIDDLE SCHOOL

241 Oneida Way, San Francisco, CA 94112

(415) 586-0840

Denman is a magnet school focusing on orchestra, choir, drama, band, dance, art and video. The magnet school also provides an after-school arts program for all Denman students. Denman provides a strong educational program for regular, gifted, bilingual, and special needs students.

JAMES LICK MIDDLE SCHOOL

1220 Noe Street, San Francisco, CA 94114

(415) 648-8080

A variety of programs has been implemented to enhance and support the traditional programs of language arts, mathematics, and reading. The overall program places additional emphasis on improving student academics in all classes and a rigorous elective curriculum. Along with the desire for higher academic achievement for all students, the school focuses on integration and the social growth of every student.

LAWTON ALTERNATIVE SCHOOL

(K to eight)

1570 31st Avenue, San Francisco, CA 94122

(415) 564-5500

See "ELEMENTARY SCHOOLS."

LUTHER BURBANK MIDDLE SCHOOL

325 La Grande Avenue, San Francisco, CA 94112

(415) 586-1650

Burbank, a marine science magnet school, has received special funding for the intensive study of oceans and marine life. Field trips and hands-on science activities are featured throughout the school curriculum. Academic excellence and high expectations are stressed for the high school-bound student. Burbank features the only award winning marching band in the City and offers an excellent orchestra and elective program.

MARINA MIDDLE SCHOOL

3500 Fillmore Street, San Francisco, CA 94123

(415) 565-9577

Marina offers a strong, academic curriculum supported and balanced by a consistently enforced discipline policy, a student leadership program, parent and community involvement, and a varied extracurricular program.

POTRERO HILL MIDDLE SCHOOL

655 DeHaro Street, San Francisco, CA 94107

(415) 647-1011

Potrero Hill's structured academic program provides basic skills in language arts, mathematics, reading, social studies, and science. Our enrichment activities include a computer lab, instrumental music, shop and art classes, a leadership class, and a drama program. An active tutorial program is available before school, at noon, and after school. Potrero Hill is committed to improving academic achievement and ethnic and racial harmony.

PRESIDIO MIDDLE SCHOOL
450 30th Avenue, San Francisco, CA 94121
(415) 752-9696

Presidio offers a structured program that provides each student with a traditional academic experience is conducive to learning and creating a smooth transition to high school. A core sixth and seventh grade academic program, band, orchestra, and unified arts are the cornerstones of our interdisciplinary approach to learning. Electives, including Spanish and French, are offered in the eighth grade. Presidio also offers an honors program and bilingual and ESL classes.

ROOSEVELT MIDDLE SCHOOL
460 Arguello Boulevard, San Francisco, CA 94118
(415) 386-1600

Roosevelt is a traditional middle school emphasizing in each student a love and desire for learning. All of our students are required to take three years of English and math, two and one-half years of science and social studies, and one year of reading. Eighth graders participate in full music and French programs. We offer an active counseling component that teaches social skills and responsibilities, recreational activities, and physical fitness.

SAN FRANCISCO COMMUNITY ALTERNATIVE SCHOOL
(K to eight)
125 Excelsior Street, San Francisco, CA 94112
(415) 239-1870
See "**ELEMENTARY SCHOOLS**."

VISITACION VALLEY MIDDLE SCHOOL
450 Raymond Avenue, San Francisco, CA 94134
(415) 239-6550

Visitacion Valley offers an extensive environmental education program that includes a week at Caritas Creek Camp for grades six and seven. The school also boasts an integrated computer curriculum with two networked computer labs staffed by two resource teachers. A tutorial program for all students is available mornings and after school.

High Schools

ABRAHAM LINCOLN HIGH SCHOOL

2162 - 24th Avenue (between Quintara and Rivera), San Francisco, CA 94116
(415) 566-1618

Lincoln prepares students for further education or entry into the job market.
The curriculum offers advanced placement and honors programs, an Academy of
Finance (a two-year program that includes finance, accounting, and computer
science, in addition to the required curriculum), foreign languages, and creative
arts.

ALAMO PARK HIGH SCHOOL

1099 Hayes Street (at Pierce), San Francisco, CA 94117
(415) 565-9756

•**Principal:** Yvonne Scarlet-Golden
   Alamo Park High School was founded in 1980. It is a small high school with
an enrollment of 200 students in grades nine through twelve. School hours are
from 8:30 a.m. to 3:10 p.m.
•**Philosophy/Goals/Curriculum:** "The school employs a unique teaching system
based on a triad—teachers, students, and parents forming a close, cooperative
network. This concept has pointed education in a new direction. Through this
learning, training, and parenting exchange, students have reached a level of
scholastic achievement they have never before experienced.

   "The school provides an option for students who desire flexible scheduling,
personal intruction, career and academic counseling or an opportunity to acceler-
ate credit requirements. The program, open to students 15 years or older, develops
academic skills at all levels of instruction. It is specifically designed to accommodate those returning to school after a prolonged absence, who lack the required
credits for graduation, who need a work-study program, or who plan to pursue a

post secondary education.

"The faculty at Alamo Park believes in teaching the basics. Whether it's teaching computer science, survival skills in the workplace, or poring over theories in street law, the teachers at Alamo Park strongly encourage their students to compete, to win and to feel good about winning.

"All parents are encouraged to volunteer several hours a month, working with the staff and assisting with students' learning activities.

"The curriculum at Alamo Park includes courses in English, Social Science, mathematics, science, business, foreign language, and electives and inter-school activities including art, dance, drama and sports.

"Special projects include a McKesson/Alamo Corporate Partnership Program, a valuable resource in increasing employability and teaching students how to live in the 'real' world; The Learning Exchange, an expansion of the tutorial program; and The Work Experience Program."

•**Admission Requirements and Procedure:** Applications for admission to Alamo Park High School are accepted all year. On site interviews are conducted for potential students.

BALBOA HIGH SCHOOL

1000 Cayuga Avenue (between Onondega and Seneca), San Francisco, CA 94112 (415) 333-2777

In addition to a comprehensive academic program, Balboa High School offers supplemental instructional services in the basic skills areas to provide for students with special needs. The range of special programs includes a computer-assisted instruction lab, a teen health clinic, and a College/Career Center.

BAY HIGH SCHOOL

700 Font Boulevard (housed in Louise Lombard School), San Francisco, CA 94123 (415) 334-0115

Bay primarily services specific group-home students who have been assigned to Bay Alternative because of their educational and behavioral needs.

DOWNTOWN SENIOR HIGH SCHOOL

110 Bartlett Street (between 22nd and 23rd streets), San Francisco, CA 94110
(415) 565-9610

•**Principal:** Lee Diamond

The Board of Education directed Emil Anderson to establish the Downtown Senior High School in 1968. It has been at its present location since 1980 and is designated a "Small High School." School hours are 8:45 a.m. to 3:15 p.m.

•**Philosophy/Goals/Curriculum:** The educational philosophy of Downtown Senior High School is permanent, yet it is also sensitive to the changing needs of students. The school began as a drop-out prevention program. It has since evolved into a model school attracting students from all parts of the city.

"We are committed advocates of our students in their academic, personal, or social endeavors. We are committed to the students' potential for growth and excellence in their academic pursuits. We are committed to preparing and recommending all students for part-time employment, and/or being a volunteer for community service. We are committed to offering our students personalized instruction based on diagnostic evaluation.

"We are committed to offering a personalized counseling program for all our students. To the student who, for whatever reason, may be disenchanted with the large comprehensive high school, we offer the alternative of a small setting together with personalized instruction. To the student who may be thinking of dropping out, we offer an opportunity for accelerated credits in a half-day program. To the student who needs to catch up on the basics, we offer an intensified basic skills program. To the student who needs to work in order to help support the family, we offer a work-experience program with a flexible schedule."

•**Admission Requirements and Procedure:** Students must complete an enrollment application signed by the student and parent. A copy of health records, test scores, and transcripts are required. Tests are required: a 40-minute diagnostic test in reading, writing, and mathematics. A parent/student conference is scheduled as well.

FRANCIS SCOTT KEY LEARNING CENTER

1350 43rd Avenue (between Irving and Judah), San Francisco, CA 94122
(415) 664-1192

Francis Scott Key Learning Center is a small, special education high school. Individualized classes leading to a high school diploma are offered to students in grades nine through twelve.

GALILEO HIGH SCHOOL

1150 Francisco Street (between Van Ness and Polk), San Francisco, CA 94109
(415) 771-3150

Galileo provides opportunities for excellence in English, mathematics, science, foreign languages, and vocational education. Honors and advance placement coursework is offered in all academic areas and is enhanced by an outstanding computer program.

GEORGE WASHINGTON HIGH SCHOOL

600 32nd Avenue (between Balboa and Clement), San Francisco, CA 94121
(415) 387-0550

Washington has a comprehensive curriculum and over 40 extracurricular clubs and organizations available to students. Special programs are provided for ESL, gifted, and special education students. Honors and advanced placement courses are also available.

INDEPENDENCE HIGH SCHOOL

A Center for Independent Study
3045 Santiago Street (between 41st and 42nd avenues), San Francisco, CA
94116
(415) 564-7717

•**Principal:** Jennie Chin-Low
Independence High School, a Center for Independent Study, opened its doors in 1980, and has an enrollment of 500 students from 15 to 20 years of age. School hours are from 8:15 a.m. to 2:35 p.m. The student must meet with the supervising teacher at a scheduled meeting at least once a week (exceptions include students on travel contracts, home study, sick leave and special assignments). A dress code is enforced.

•**Philosophy/Goals/Curriculum:** Independence High School "personalizes student learning and offers an educational program which insures that each student has the opportunity to develop to the fullest of his or her individual potential. It offers a varied curriculum and many resources to achieve this goal. The Center offers a full educational program for ninth through twelfth grade students. Its student body comes from all over the city and from other school districts. The basic instructional program of the Center is supplemented by programs sponsored by the Recreation Department, Red Cross, museums, and community-based programs.

"The students' academic work is based on independent study contracts agreed to by both the students and the supervising teachers. Students at CFIS can complete credits for a regular high school diploma. The course work completed at CFIS can be transferred to other schools. It can be used to fulfill college entrance requirements. Independence High School also offers preparation for the CHSPE; concentrated study in basic skills; GED preparation; vocational exploration and survival skills for the world of work."

•**Admission Requirements and Procedure:** High school students must have a referral from a school counselor. Minor students must also have parental consent.

INTERNATIONAL STUDIES ACADEMY

693 Vermont Street (Potrero Hill area), San Francisco, CA 94107
(415) 695-3011

•**Principal:** Steve Hirabayashi

The International Studies Academy, founded in 1982, has developed a special magnet program that focuses on global perspectives and prepares students to live and work in an international community. Enrollment is at 500 for students grades nine through twelve. Average class size is 30 with 20 full-time and ten part-time teachers, all of whom are credentialed. School hours are 8:30 a.m. to 3:30 p.m. The school is specially equipped for teaching the hearing impaired.

Accredited by WASC.

•**Philosophy/Goals/Curriculum:** International Studies Academy has a strong academic curriculum and a faculty that gives students the support to meet the challenge of the rigorous classes. I.S.A. has devised classes that help students improve academic skills as well as broaden their perspectives about the importance of education and, particularly, international education.

I.S.A. emphasizes foreign language and social studies in order for students to fully participate in an internationally interdependent world. The Foreign Language Program now consists of German, French, Chinese, Japanese, and Spanish classes. Students use the Foreign Language lab which includes computer technology and video as well as an audiolingual approach.

I.S.A. has a state-of-the-art computer laboratory. Over 30 Macintosh SE's are used for instructional support in all subjects. Students use the computers to support classroom activities, publish newsletters, and create spread sheets. The video center includes new editing equipment. The school trains students as well as teachers in use of the equipment. Classroom productions have been taped and sent to other countries as video exchange letters.

Through an internship program, juniors and seniors work at international businesses and service organizations once a week in order to gain skills in the working world, an entrance that could never be duplicated in the classroom .

The Great Decisions program, sponsored by the World Affairs Council, allows students to become involved in current international events.

J. EUGENE McATEER HIGH SCHOOL

555 Portola Drive, San Francisco, CA 94131

(415) 824-6001

Students in a well integrated student body take a demanding and structured academic program at McAteer. Students may also take specialized instruction in the School of Arts, ESL/bilingual and special education programs, alternative learning (ALTA), Urban Pioneers, physical education, Naval ROTC, business, and practical arts.

JOHN O'CONNELL SCHOOL of TECHNOLOGY

2905 21st Street (between Harrison and Treat), San Francisco, CA 94110

(415) 648-1326

Industrial/technical training is available in conjunction with a high school diploma. For the university-bound, a full range of college preparatory courses is now available. New for 1988 - 89 is a one-of-a-kind college preparatory program in pre-engineering, emphasizing specialization in electronic, mechanical, aeronautic, and architectural programs.

LOUISE M. LOMBARD HIGH SCHOOL
700 Font Boulevard (at Tapia), San Francisco, CA 94132
(415) 586-4488

Louise Lombard is a school for special education students through age 21. It is for students who have not been able to adjust or function in a regular high school setting.

LOWELL HIGH SCHOOL
1101 Eucalyptus Drive (at Forest View), San Francisco CA 94132
(415) 566-7900

•**Principal:** Dr. Alan Fibish

Lowell High School was founded in 1856. It is a four-year high school, enrolling approximately 3,000 students. School hours are from 7:40 a.m. to 3:20 p.m.

•**Philosophy/Goals/Curriculum:** "The primary function of Lowell High School is to offer the young people of San Francisco their traditional choice of attending a special non-districted secondary school emphasizing college preparation in the academic disciplines.

"Lowell's curricular and co-curricular programs offer a wide range of opportunities for personal and intellectual growth. They are designed to provide every Lowell student with a well-rounded liberal education which will prepare him for entrance to the college of his choice and to the world of adult living. A fundamental premise in administering the school is that Lowell students conduct themselves with a degree of responsibility that permits great latitude in self-direction and in self-discipline. Such dependability allows maximum use of individual decision-making in planning school careers.

"Features of the instructional program include a modified modular schedule, resource centers, choice of teachers, and self-scheduled time. Subject offerings are diverse and rigorous with all students taking four academic subjects each semester. Honors classes have been designed especially for students who show exceptional ability in specific subject fields. College level Advanced Placement courses are

offered in all subject areas and are taught in compliance with College Entrance
Examination Board standards. An outstanding Creative and Performing Arts
Department fosters the aesthetic and cultural well-being of students while their
physical welfare is promoted by a skill-building physical education program leading
to team sports and to extensive Girls' Athletic Association activities.

"Complementing the curriculum is a co-curricular program of unique educational scope and worth. It provides opportunity for decision making over a wide
range of activities, from organizing rooting sections and producing rallies to
sponsoring outside speakers and teaching mini-courses. Lowell students are
guaranteed the widest possible latitude within policy and legal limits to devise
their own student government, develop their budgets, and stand on their own
decisions."

•**Admission Requirements and Procedures:** Admission is based on seventh and
eighth grade scholastic achievement in English, mathematics, science and social
studies, plus composite score on the CTBS. The 700 applicants with the best
aggregate scores (combining grades and CTBS) are admitted. Tenth and eleventh
grade admissions are based on marks in the previous year (minimum grade point
average of 3.60 to be eligible).

MARK TWAIN ALTERNATIVE HIGH SCHOOL

1541 - 12th Avenue (between Kirkham and Lawton), San Francisco, CA 94122
(415) 731-3380

•**Administrator:** John Q. Lucero

Mark Twain High School is a "small high school" that was founded in 1981. It
has 180 students in grades nine through twelve. School hours are 8:30 a.m. to
3:10 p.m.

•**Philosophy/Goals/Curriculum:** "The school philosophy is a working philosophy. It provides for a small class size; teacher-student ratio is 1:10. It offers
personalized instruction (diagnostic/prescriptive) and provides the educational
requirements for a high school diploma. Each student is expected to have an 80
percent plus attendance record, maintain a grade point average of 2.0, and
cooperate with all individuals.

"Mark Twain High School recognizes individual differences, provides for
promotion any time during the school year (variable credit system), and provides a
psychological environment based on student pride, reward and success. A flexible

school structure attempts to maximize the potential of all students. There are intensive guidance services focusing upon personal, social, emotional, and work-study programs; and the opportunity for parent participation (parent conferences/meetings). The school also provides a strong adult-to-student counseling component."

MISSION HIGH SCHOOL

3750 18th Street (between Dolores and Church), San Francisco, CA 94114
(415) 241-6240

Mission provides a comprehensive academic curriculum that emphasizes student achievement and success. Special site programs include the following: GATE, advanced placement classes, special education, Step to College, Mission to College/UCO, SAT preparation, and bilingual/LEP.

NEWCOMER HIGH SCHOOL

2340 Jackson Street (between Webster and Fillmore), San Francisco, CA 94115
(415) 241-6584

•**Principal:** Paul Cheng
Newcomer High School was created in 1979 by the San Francisco Board of Education with the purpose of providing a transitional educational program for foreign born, high school age (14 to 17) students who do not have adequate fluency in English. There are 550 students enrolled in grades nine to eleven. School hours are from 8:00 a.m. to 3:11 p.m. There is a dress code.
•**Philosophy/Goals/Curriculum:** "Students are provided intensive instruction in English as a Second Language (ESL) and bilingual support subject classes such as social studies, mathematics, and electives that promote continued acquisition of basic academic skills and concepts. In the bilingual support classes the student's primary language as well as English is used. The students can remain at Newcomer High School for a maximum of one year.

"When a student does not belong to one of the major language groups, he or she is placed in individualized subject classes where English and the student's primary language (where possible) are utilized. BILP students take their ESL classes in an integrated setting with other students. A limited selection of other required/elective courses is available, including physical education, art, biology, life science, typing/business skills, and introduction to computers. All students take part in state and district testing programs. Because students enroll on a continuous basis, Newcomer has a variable credit policy."

PHILLIP AND SALA BURTON HIGH SCHOOL

45 Conkling Street (between Silver and Bayshore), San Francisco, CA 94124
(415) 826-9090

Burton offers a college preparatory program that stresses high academic standards and student achievement. The basic curriculum is enhanced by an outstanding computer program. Graduation requirements meet and exceed university prerequisites.

RAOUL WALLENBERG TRADITIONAL HIGH SCHOOL

40 Vega Street (at O'Farrell), San Francisco, CA 94115
(415) 346-7466

•**Principal:** Helen McKenna
Wallenberg Traditional High School, founded in 1981, is an alternative public high school offering a college preparatory program. It presently serves 615 students in grades nine through twelve. School hours are from 8:00 a.m to 3:02 p.m. There is a dress code.
•**Philosophy/Goals/Curriculum:** "Wallenberg offers students the opportunity to study a college preparatory program within an academic atmosphere in a small school organized and supervised in a traditional manner. Traditional aspects include a dress code, observance of time-honored customs, adherence to study, good citizenship, and an honor system. The required program for all ninth grade students at Wallenberg includes four academic subjects, physical education, and an elective. Since algebra and a foreign language are required, it is highly recommended that incoming students have the potential to perform at grade level in mathematics and in English."
•**Admission Requirements and Procedure:** "1) A signed commitment to the philosophy of the school by the parents. 2) A desire on the part of students to study academic subjects and to accede to behavior and dress codes. 3) Initial

application. 4) Attendance at one of several night meetings for both students and parents. 5) An interview. Prospective students should place their names on the list for Wallenberg as early as possible."

SAN FRANCISCO SCHOOL OF THE ARTS

555 Portola Drive (at O'Shaughnessy), San Francisco, CA 94131
(415) 550-1566

• **Administrator:** Daniel Ryan

The School of the Arts opened its doors to 280 students in September 1982. It serves grades nine through twelve. School hours are from 8:55 a.m. to 3:00 p.m.

• **Philosophy/Goals/Curriculum:** "The School of the Arts is a magnet school inaugurated at McAteer High School to provide students with the opportunity for a comprehensive academic education in addition to intensive pre-professional training in one of four arts disciplines: music, dance, visual arts, and theater. Time beyond the regular school day is necessary for additional art activities.

"Students will have the opportunity to develop to their fullest potential. The School program will be established with the following objectives: to develop talent and skills in visual art, dance, music, or theater and related fields; to prepare academically for further study in college, university, conservatory or professional school; and to obtain an understanding of the relationships among the arts and an appreciation of cultural activities. Parent cooperation is essential for student participation in the School of the Arts program."

• **Admission Requirements and Procedure:** Prospective students are given an audition and personal interview. Grades are also considered.

SCHOOL FOR BUSINESS AND COMMERCE

350 Broadway (between Sansome and Montgomery), San Francisco, CA 94133
(415) 241-6595

High school graduation requirements may be met through courses such as word processing, data entry, banking, accounting, small business management/ownership, food services, and cosmetology. High school students attend either morning or afternoon sessions. A summer session is available to all students.

SUNSHINE CONTINUATION HIGH SCHOOL

2730 Bryant Street, San Francisco, CA 94110

(415) 695-2461

•**Principal:** Mrs. Eldoris C. Cameron

Sunshine has a variable credit system, diagnostic-prescriptive individualized instruction, a maximum class size of 22 students, and an emphasis on a work study program. All students have an opportunity to earn a regular high school diploma.

WOODROW WILSON HIGH SCHOOL

400 Mansell Street (between Somerset and Bowdoin), San Francisco, CA 94134

(415) 239-6200

Woodrow Wilson High School focuses on a comprehensive academic instructional program that emphasizes student achievement. Special school programs include music, art, and computer instruction.

Public Schools
MARIN COUNTY

PUBLIC SCHOOL DISTRICTS IN MARIN COUNTY

Marin County public education is administered through a number of small districts. The school serving each child is determined by the location of that child's home.

Your local neighborhood school should be contacted for information on enrollment.

Children who may qualify for special education services should be referred to the Resource Specialist at your local school. After an assessment of needs, the child will be placed in an appropriate program.

Following is a list of the Marin public school districts and their telephone numbers:

Bolinas-Stinson Union School District: 868-1603.

Dixie School District (San Rafael): 479-8881.

Kentfield School District: 461-2880.

Laguna Joint School District (K through sixth) (Petaluma): (707) 762-6051.

Lagunitas School District: 488-9399.

Larkspur School District: 924-0345.

Lincoln School District (K through sixth) (Petaluma): (707) 763-0045.

Mill Valley School District: 389-7700.

Nicasio School District (K through eighth): 662-2184

Novato Unified School District: 897-4201

Reed Union School District (Tiburon): 381-1281.

Ross School District (K through eighth): 457-2705.

Ross Valley School District (San Anselmo and Fairfax): 454-2162.

San Rafael Elementary and High School Districts: 485-2300.

Sausalito School District: 332-3190.

Shoreline Unified School District (Tomales/Pt. Reyes/Inverness/Bodega): (707) 878-2266.

Appendix I

The following is a list of private schools that did not submit detailed descriptions.

ALL HALLOWS SCHOOL
1601 Lane Street, San Francisco, CA 94124
(415) 822-8780
•**Principal:** Sister Marie Jeanne Gaillac

CORPUS CHRISTI SCHOOL
75 Francis Street, San Francisco, CA 94112
(415) 587-7014
•**Principal:** Sister Fernanda Rossi

EPIPHANY SCHOOL
600 Italy Avenue, San Francisco, CA 94112
(415) 587-6900
•**Principal:** Sister Rita Marie Jovick

IMMACULATE CONCEPTION ELEMENTARY SCHOOL
1550 Treat Avenue, San Francisco, CA 94110
(415) 824-6860
•**Principal:** Sister Jonelle Keating

MISSION DOLORES SCHOOL
3371 16th Street, San Francisco, CA 94114
(415) 861-7673
•**Principal:** Sister Louise O'Reilly

OUR LADY OF LORETTO SCHOOL
1811 Virginia Avenue, Novato, CA 94947
(415) 892-5757

OUR LADY OF THE VISITACION SCHOOL
785 Sunnydale Avenue, San Francisco, CA 94134
(415) 239-7840
•**Principal:** Sister Donna Kramer

ST. ANNE SCHOOL
1320 - 14th Avenue, San Francisco, CA 94122
(415) 664-7977
•**Principal:** Sister Esther McEgan

ST. BRIGID SCHOOL
2250 Franklin Street, San Francisco, CA 94109
(415) 673-4523
•**Principal:** Sister Carmen Santiuste

ST. CECILIA SCHOOL
660 Vicente Street, San Francisco, CA 94116
(415) 731-8400
•**Principal:** Sister Marilyn Murphy

ST. CHARLES SCHOOL
3250-18th Street, San Francisco, CA 94110
(415) 861-7652
•**Principal:** Sister Mary Matthew Brazil

ST. ELIZABETH SCHOOL
450 Somerset Street, San Francisco, CA 94134
(415) 468-3247
•**Principal:** Mary F. Lyons

ST. FINN BARR SCHOOL
419 Hearst Avenue, San Francisco, CA 94112
(415) 333-1800
•**Principal:** Sister Ita Murray

ST. JAMES SCHOOL
321 Fair Oaks Street, San Francisco, CA 94110
(415) 647-8972
•**Principal:** Sister Elizabeth Murray

ST. MARY CHINESE DAY SCHOOL
902 Stockton Street, San Francisco, CA 94108
(415) 362-7394
•**Principal:** Mrs. Evelyn Hall

ST. MICHAEL SCHOOL
55 Farallones Street, San Francisco, CA 94112
(415) 585-4781
•**Principal:** Paul Lux

ST. PATRICK'S
120 King Street, Larkspur, CA 94939
(415) 924-0501

ST. PAUL ELEMENTARY SCHOOL
1660 Church Street, San Francisco, CA 94131
(415) 648-2055; (415) 647-2525
•**Principal:** Sister Eileen Healy

ST. PAUL OF THE SHIPWRECK SCHOOL
6475 3rd Street, San Francisco, CA 94124
(415) 467-1798
•**Principal:** Mrs. Ruth Perry

SS. PETER & PAUL SCHOOL
632 Filbert Street, San Francisco, CA 94133
(415) 421-5219
•**Principal:** Sister Barbara Campbell

ST. PETER SCHOOL
1266 Florida Street, San Francisco, CA 94110
(415) 647-8662
•**Principal:** Sister Rosann Fraher

ST. PHILIP SCHOOL
665 Elizabeth Street, San Francisco, CA 94114
(415) 824-8467
•**Principal:** Sister Patricia Lynch

ST. STEPHEN SCHOOL
401 Eucalyptus Drive, San Francisco, CA 94132
(415) 664-8331
•**Principal:** Sister Paulina Simms

ST. THOMAS MORE SCHOOL
50 Thomas More Way, San Francisco, CA 94132
(415) 337-0100
•**Principal:** Joseph T. Elsbernd

ST. VINCENT DE PAUL SCHOOL
2350 Green Street, San Francisco, CA 94123
(415) 346-5505
•**Principal:** George Enes

Appendix II

SAN FRANCISCO PRIMARY SCHOOLS

1. Independent
Children's Day School
Katherine Michiels School
Mother Goose School Inc.
One Fifty Parker Street School
Pacific Primary School

2. Montessori
Big City Montessori School
Binet-Montessori School
Montessori House of Children
The San Francisco School

3. Church Affiliated
Cornerstone Academy/Little
Lights School
Lakeside Presbyterian Center for
Children

SAN FRANCISCO ELEMENTARY AND MIDDLE SCHOOLS

1. Independent
Adda Clevenger Junior Preparatory
and Theater School for Children

Cathedral School for Boys
The Children's School of San
Francisco
Discovery Center School
Fellowship Academy
French American International
School
Hamlin School
Hillwood Academic Day School
Katherine Delmar Burke School
Kittredge School
The Laurel School
Live Oak School
Lycee Francais French School
The Phoenix Academy
Presidio Hill School
Rivendell School
San Francisco Chinese Parents'
Committee School
San Francisco Day School
The San Francisco School
The San Francisco Waldorf School
Synergy School
Town School

2. Montessori
Big City Montessori School
Binet-Montessori School
The Children's School of San

Francisco
Maria Montessori School of the
   Golden Gate
Montessori House of Children

3. **Religiously Affiliated**
   Other than Roman Catholic
   Brandeis-Hillel Day School
   Cathedral School for Boys
   Cornerstone Academy
   Fellowship Academy
   Hebrew Academy of San Francisco
   International Christian School
   St. Paulus Lutheran School
   San Francisco Junior Academy
   West Portal Lutheran School
   Zion Lutheran School

4. **Roman Catholic**
   Convent of the Sacred Heart
      Elementary School
   Ecole Notre Dame des Victoires
   Holy Name of Jesus School
   Sacred Heart Grammar School
   St. Anthony's School
   St. Dominic School
   St. Emydius School
   St. Gabriel Parish School
   St. John's Elementary School
   St. Joseph School
   St. Monica School
   St. Thomas the Apostle School
   Schools of the Sacred Heart
   Star of the Sea School
   Stuart Hall for Boys

SAN FRANCISCO HIGH SCHOOLS

1. **Independent**
   Drew College Preparatory School
   Lick-Wilmerding High School
   Morrisania West, Inc. (S.F. Postal
      Street Academy)
   New Learning School
   San Francisco University High
      School
   The Urban School of San Francisco
   Wildshaw International School

2. **Religiously Affiliated**
   Other than Roman Catholic
   Bridgemont High School

3. **Roman Catholic**
   Convent of the Sacred Heart High
      School
   Immaculate Conception Academy
   Mercy High School
   Presentation High School
   Archbishop Riordon High School
   Sacred Heart Cathedral Preparatory
   St. Ignatius College Preparatory
      School
   St. John Ursuline High School
   St. Paul's High School
   St. Rose Academy

4. **Special Education in San Francisco**
   Private Schools
   Burt Center

Challenge to Learning
Edgewood Children's Center
Edgewood Day Treatment
Erikson School
Hergl School
Jamestown Learning Center
La Mel School
Oakes Children's Center
The Open Book School
San Francisco Hearing and Speech
    Center
Sandpaths Academy
Sterne School

SAN FRANCISCO
PUBLIC SCHOOLS

1. **Elementary Schools**
    Alamo Elementary School
    Alvarado Elementary School
    Argonne Alternative School
    Bessie Carmichael School
    Bret Harte School
    Bryant School
    Buena Vista Alternative School
    Cabrillo School
    Claire Lilienthal Alternative
        School
    Clarendon Alternative School
    Cleveland School
    Commodore Sloat School
    Daniel Webster School
    Dr. Charles Drew Alternative
        School
    Douglas Traditional Alternative

School
Edison School
El Dorado School
Fairmount School
Filipino Education Center
Francis Scott Key Elementary
    School
Frank McCoppin School
Garfield School
George Peabody School
George R. Moscone School
George Washington Carver School
Glen Park School
Golden Gate School
Grattan School
Guadalupe School
Hillcrest School
Jean Parker School
Jefferson School
John Muir School
John Swett Alternative School
Junipero Serra School
Lafayette School
Lakeshore Alternative School
Lawton Alternative School
Leonard R. Flynn School
Longfellow School
Marshall School
McKinley School
Miraloma School
Mission Education Center
Monroe School
New Traditions School
Paul Revere School
Raphael Weill School

Redding School
Robert L. Stevenson School
Rooftop Alternative School
San Francisco Community Alternative School
Sanchez School
Sheridan School
Sherman School
Sir Francis Drake School
Spring Valley School
Starr King School
Sutro School
Ulloa School
Visitacion Valley School
West Portal School
William R. De Avila School
Yick Wo Alternative Elementary School

2. **Middle Schools**
A. P. Giannini Middle School
Aptos Middle School
Benjamin Franklin Middle School
Dr. Martin Luther King, Jr. Alternative School
Everett Middle School
Francisco Middle School
Herbert Hoover Middle School
Horace Mann Alternative School
James Denman Middle School
James Lick Middle School
Lawton Alternative School
Luther Burbank Middle School
Marina Middle School
Potrero Hill Middle School

Presidio Middle School
Roosevelt Middle School
San Francisco Community Alternative School
Visitacion Valley Middle School

3. **High Schools**
Abraham Lincoln High School
Alamo Park High School
Balboa High School
Bay High School
Downtown Senior High School
Francis Scott Key Learning Center
Galileo High School
George Washington High School
Independence High School
International Studies Academy
J. Eugene McAteer High School
John O'Connell School of Technology
Louise M. Lombard High School
Lowell High School
Mark Twain Alternative High School
Mission High School
Newcomer High School
Phillip and Sala Burton High School
Raoul Wallenberg Traditional High School
San Francisco School of the Arts
School for Business and Commerce
Sunshine Continuation High School
Woodrow Wilson High School

MARIN COUNTY ELEMENTARY AND MIDDLE SCHOOLS

1. Independent
Cascade Canyon School
Children's Circle Center
Kaleidoscope School
Lycee Francais International
Marin Country Day School
Marin Primary School
Marin Waldorf School
Mount Tamalpais School
Real School
Tam Creek School

2. Montessori
Marin Horizon School
Sparrow Creek Montessori School

3. Religiously Affiliated
Other than Roman Catholic
Brandeis-Hillel Day School
Christian Life School
Open Door Christian School

4. Roman Catholic
St. Anselm's School
St. Hilary School
St. Mark's School
St. Raphael's School
St. Rita School
San Domenico Early Education
  School
San Domenico Lower School

MARIN COUNTY HIGH SCHOOLS

Branson School
Marin Academy
Marin Catholic High School
North Bay Marin School
San Domenico High School

MARIN COUNTY SPECIAL EDUCATION

Allaire School
Child Center
LeeBil School
Marin School for Learning
Sky's the Limit
Sunny Hills Children's Services
Timothy Murphy School

San Francisco Maps

Location almost always plays an important role in determining the choice of a school. In San Francisco the private schools are scattered throughout the city and finding them can be a frustrating task. The following maps are provided to enable the reader to pinpoint areas in which private schools of particular interest can be found. The San Francisco Unified School District has maps of its elementary, middle, and high schools available through the General Services Office, 135 Van Ness Avenue. Phone 241-6000 to make certain the map you want is available.

SCHOOL LISTING FOR MAP 1

Number   School Name and Address

1	Adda Clevenger Junior Preparatory and Theater School for Children, Mid-Sunset at 34th Avenue
13	Cornerstone Academy (R), 1925 Lawton Street (25th Avenue)
23	Hebrew Academy of San Francisco (R), 645 14th Avenue (Balboa)
26	Holy Name of Jesus School (C), 1560 40th Avenue (Lawton/40th Avenue)
30	Katherine Delmar Burke, 7070 California Street (32nd Avenue)
32	Kittredge School, 2355 Lake Street (25th Avenue)
38	Lycee Francais-French School, 3301 Balboa Street (34th Avenue)
43	Mother Goose School Inc., 334 28th Avenue (California/Clement)
53	Rivendell School, 4501 Irving Street (46th Avenue)
71	St. Monica School (C), 5020 Geary Blvd. (24th Avenue)
74	St. Thomas the Apostle (C), 3801 Balboa Street (39th Avenue)

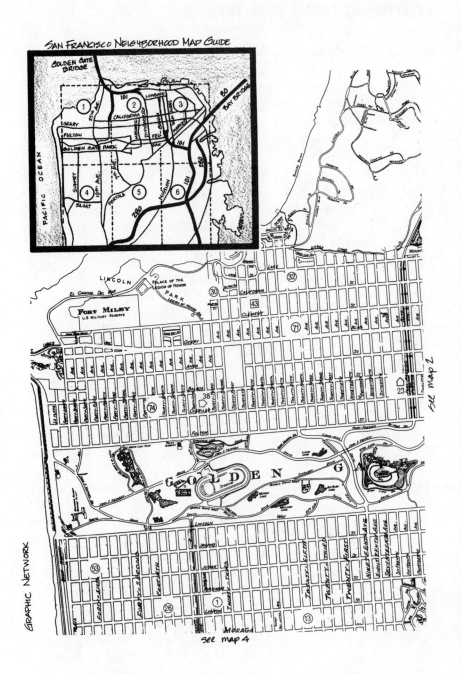

MAP LEGEND:
O = Elementary and Middle School; □ = Primary School; ▲ = High School; ◆ = Special Education School; C = Catholic School;
R = Religiously Affiliated School; ▷ = Multi-grade level School

SCHOOL LISTING FOR MAP 2

Number	School Name and Address
6	Burt Center, 940 Grove Street (Steiner)
8	Challenge to Learning, 924 Balboa Street (10th Avenue)
11	Convent of the Sacred Heart **(C)**, 2222 Broadway (Webster/Fillmore)
12	Convent of the Sacred Heart High School **(C)**, 2222 Broadway (Webster/Fillmore)
15	Drew College Preparatory School, 2901 California Street (Broderick)
22	Hamlin School, 2120 Broadway (Webster/Buchanan)
25	Hillwood Academic School, 2521 Scott Street (Broadway/Pacific)
35	The Laurel School, 350 9th Avenue (Geary/Clement)
37	Live Oak School, 117 Diamond Street (18th Street)
42	Morrisania West Inc., San Francisco Postal Street Academy 914 Divisadero Street (McAllister/Eddy)
45	Oakes Children's Center, 1348 10th Avenue (Irving/Judah)
46	One Fifty Parker Street, 150 Parker Avenue (Geary/Euclid)
47	The Open Book School, 2031 Bush Street (Buchanan/Webster)
48	Pacific Primary School, 1500 Grove Street (Baker)
50	Presentation High School **(C)**, 2350 Turk Street (Masonic)
51	Presidio Hill School, 3839 Washington Street (Maple/Cherry)
55	Sacred Heart Grammar **(C)**, 735 Fell Street (Fillmore)
65	St. Dominic School **(C)**, 2445 Pine Street (Pierce/Steiner)
57	San Francisco Day School, 350 Masonic Avenue (Golden Gate)
58	San Francisco Hearing and Speech Center, 1234 Divisadero Street (Ellis/Eddy)
61	San Francisco University High School, 3065 Jackson Street (Baker/Lyon)
62	The San Francisco Waldorf School, 2938 Washington Street (Broderick/Divisadero)
75	Star of the Sea School **(C)**, 360 9th Avenue (Geary Boulevard)
76	Sterne School, 2690 Jackson Street (Scott)
77	Stuart Hall for Boys **(C)**, 2252 Broadway (Fillmore/Webster)
78	Synergy School, 975 Grove Street (Steiner)
79	Town School, 2750 Jackson Street (Scott)
80	The Urban School of San Francisco, 1563 Page Street (Masonic/Ashbury)
83	Zion Lutheran School **(R)**, 495 9th Avenue (Geary/ Anza)

see map 1

see map 3

see map 5

MAP LEGEND:
○ = Elementary and Middle School; □ = Primary School; ▲ = High School; ◆ = Special Education School; C = Catholic School;
R = Religiously Affiliated School; ▷ = Multi-grade level School

SCHOOL LISTING FOR MAP 3

Number	School Name and Address
3	Binet-Montessori School, 1715 Octavia Street (Pine)
7	Cathedral School for Boys **(R)**, 1275 Sacramento Street (Jones)
9	Children's Day School, 333 Dolores Street (16th Street)
16	Ecole Notre Dame des Victoires **(C)**, 659 Pine Street (Grant/Stockton)
21	French American International School, 220 Buchanan Street (Waller)
24	Hergl School, 1570 Greenwich Street (Franklin)
28	International Christian School **(R)**, 42 Waller Street (Octavia/Market)
29	Jamestown Learning Center, 25 14th Street (Harrison)
34	La Mel School, 1801 Bush Street (Octavia)
41	Montessori House of Children, 1187 Franklin Street (Geary)
44	New Learning School, 1016 Eddy (Gough)
49	The Phoenix Academy, 44 Page Street (Gough/Franklin)
54	Sacred Heart Cathedral Preparatory **(C),** 1055 Ellis Street (Gough/Franklin)
70	St. Joseph School **(C)**, 220 10th Street (Howard)
72	St. Paulus Lutheran School **(R)**, 888 Turk Street (Gough)
56	San Francisco Chinese Parents' Committee School, 843 Stockton Street (Clay)
63	Sandpaths Academy, 525 Bryant Street (3rd and 4th Streets)

see map 6

SCHOOL LISTING FOR MAP 4

Number	School Name and Address
17	Edgewood Children's Center, 1801 Vicente Street (29th Avenue)
18	Edgewood Day Treatment Program, 2665 28th Avenue (Vicente)
33	Lakeside Presbyterian Center for Children **(R)**, 201 Eucalyptus Drive (19th Avenue)
40	Mercy High School **(C)**, 3250 19th Avenue (Winston/Eucalyptus)
67	St. Gabriel Parish School **(C)**, 2550 41st Avenue (Ulloa/Vicente)
68	St. Ignatius College Preparatory School **(C)**, 2001 37th Avenue (Quintara)
81	West Portal Lutheran **(R)**, 200 Sloat Boulevard (19th Avenue/ Portola)

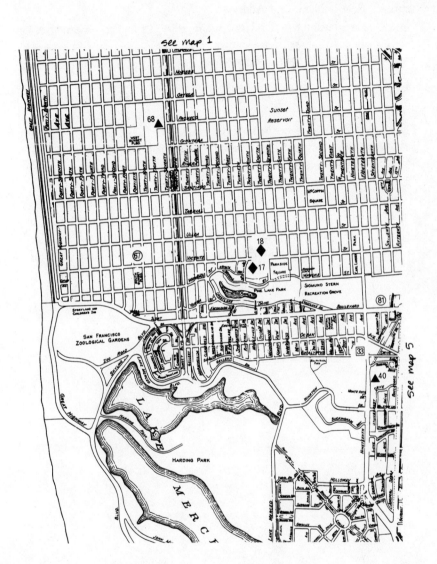

MAP LEGEND:

○ = Elementary and Middle School; □ = Primary School; ▲ = High School; ◆ = Special Education School; **C** = Catholic School; **R** = Religiously Affiliated School; ▷ = Multi-grade level School

SCHOOL LISTING FOR MAP 5

Number	School Name and Address
52	Archbishop Riordan High School **(C)**, 175 Phelan Avenue (Ocean/Judson)
4	Brandeis-Hillel Day School **(R)**, 655 Brotherhood Way (Lake Merced/19th Avenue)
10	The Children's School of San Francisco, 399 San Fernando Way (Ocean)
14	Discovery Center School, 65 Ocean Avenue (Alemany)
19	Erikson School, 333 Randolph Street (Arch Street)
36	Lick-Wilmerding High School, 755 Ocean Avenue (Howth/I-280)
39	Maria Montessori School of the Golden Gate, 678 Portola Drive (Woodside)
66	St. Emydius Elementary **(C)**, 301 De Montfort Avenue (Ocean/Jules)
69	St. John's Elementary **(C)**, 925 Chenery Street (Burnside/Chilton)
59	San Francisco Junior Academy **(R)**, 66 Geneva Avenue (Phelan/Howth)
82	Wildshaw International School, 385 Ashton Avenue (Ocean)

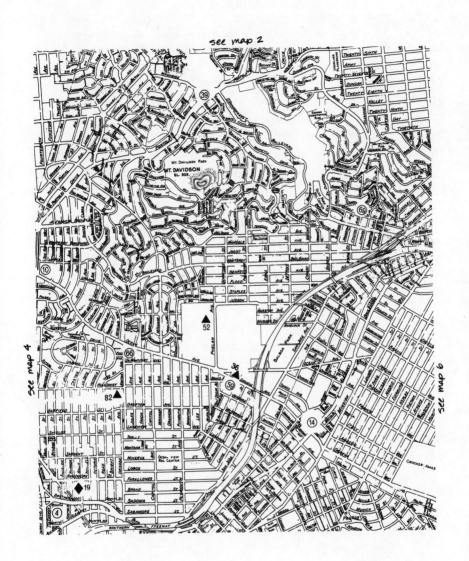

MAP LEGEND:

◯ = Elementary and Middle School; ☐ = Primary School; ▲ = High School; ◆ = Special Education School; **C** = Catholic School;
R = Religiously Affiliated School; ▷ = Multi-grade level School

SCHOOL LISTING FOR MAP 6

Number	School Name and Address
2	Big City Montessori School, 240 Industrial Street (Loomis)
5	Bridgemont High School **(R)**, 501 Cambridge Street (Felton)
20	Fellowship Academy **(R)**, 501 Cambridge Street (Felton)
27	Immaculate Conception Academy **(C)**, 3625 24th Street (Guerrero)
31	Katherine Michiels School, 1335 Guerrero (26th Street)
64	St. Anthony School **(C)**, 299 Precita Avenue (Folsom)
84	St. John Ursuline School **(C)**, 4056 Mission Street (Bosworth)
85	St. Paul's High School **(C)**, 317 29th Street (Church)
60	The San Francisco School, 300 Gaven Street (Boylston)

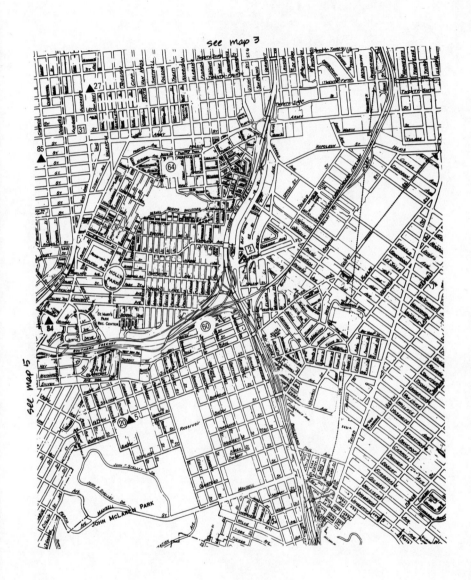

see map 3

see map 5

MAP LEGEND:

○ = Elementary and Middle School; □ = Primary School; ▲ = High School; ◆ = Special Education School; C = Catholic School;

R = Religiously Affiliated School; ▷ = Multi-grade level School

Author Biographies

DAVID DENMAN

David Denman has taught at every grade level from 7th through college, and is the former Master Teacher and Consultant on Education for the national organization of Quaker Schools and Colleges. Few educators know America's private day and boarding schools *from the inside* better than David. He has worked as a teacher or as an administrator in nine of them, and on three occasions he has been a Director of Admissions. Presently an independant educational counselor and consultant, David has school placement, college counseling and TIME OUT clientele that is nationwide.

David is the father of four children and co-author of a widely praised book, *Touching the World*, about the developmental needs of young people. Thus, a distinctive aspect of his work is arranging enriching, extraordinary summer, semester, and year-long opportunities all over the world for young people – and for people not so young. David also works with numerous young people who, for one reason or another, have gotten "off track," educationally speaking.

David is a member of the Independent Educational Consultant's Association, the National Association for College Admissions Counselors, and the National Society for Internships and Experimental Education.

VERA OBERMEYER

Vera Obermeyer, LEARNING ASSOCIATES, is an educational consultant in San Francisco. She has been in the field of education for over twenty-five years, as a teacher, counselor, and school psychologist with students from preschool to graduate school. Vera is presently in private practice as a Licensed Educational Psychologist and a Marriage, Family and Child Counselor. Her specialties are in school/class placement counseling; psychological-educational assessment; identification of gifted children and children in need of special education; and psychotherapy with individuals, couples, and families. Her services include consultation with parents and school personnel, and in-service training and staff development. Vera holds a Master's Degree in Education and Counseling, and a Ph.D. in Marital and Family Therapy. With Suzanne Warren, she co-authored the previous edition of **Finding a School for Your Child in San Francisco and Marin** and co-founded LEARNING ASSOCIATES, Educational Consultants. Vera maintains a "Clearing House" of openings in San Francisco private schools to assist parents in the educational placement of their children.

VIRGINIA REISS

Virginia Reiss holds a Master of Science degree in clinical psychology and credentials in school psychology and school administration. Her colleges include the University of California, Berkeley; and San Francisco State University. She is licensed as an Educational Psychologist.

For the past eighteen years, Virginia has worked actively with children, adolescents, and adults at all educational levels. She served with distinction in the public schools for a number of years before opening her private practice as an educational psychologist and consultant in Marin County. Virginia is recognized as an expert in determining the causes of learning difficulties, and in finding solutions which lead to happier, more productive educational experiences. She has advised numerous students and parents about school and college placement.

In order to maintain first hand knowledge of local day schools, boarding schools, colleges, and programs for children with special needs, Virginia travels extensively throughout the United States each year. Her professional affiliations include the American Psychological Association, and the Independent Educational Consultants Association.

SUZANNE WARREN

Suzanne Warren has spent more than thirty years in the field of education, both as a classroom teacher and in special education. Her experience includes more than 15 years devoted to diagnosing and remediating learning disabilities in children and adults, designing special education programs for learning disabled children, organizing and leading workshops, and writing in the field of education.

Suzanne is currently Curriculum Director at Marin Primary School in Larkspur. She holds a Master's Degree in Special Education, an Elementary Education credential, a Learning Handicapped credential, and a Resource Specialist credential. She is a professional member of Association of Educational Therapists and an avid quilter as well as a proud parent and grandparent.

Index